Sharing God's Love
in CHILDREN'S
CHURCH

A Year's Worth of Programs for Children Ages 3-7

Reproducibles Included

Lisa Flinn and Barbara Younger

Abingdon Press
Nashville

SHARING GOD'S LOVE
IN CHILDREN'S CHURCH
A Year's Worth of Programs for Children Ages 3-7

ISBN 13: 978-0-687-49165-0
PACP00334972-02

07 08 09 10 11 12 13 14 15 16 - 10 9 8 7 6 5 4 3 2 1

Manufactured in the United States of America

Dedication

For Diana Montgomery,
Thanks for sharing your love with the kids at our church.

Table of Contents

INTRODUCTION

Thanks for Sharing!

Gold stars to you for sharing your time and talents. Soon you will lead the kids at your church or preschool in discovering many happy ways to share God's love. These 52 engaging programs work for small or large groups and are designed to fit a 30-minute, 45-minute, or 60-minute schedule. The Opening, the Bible Story, the Prayer, and the Exploring Activity create a complete thirty-minute program. Just add the snack and/or "Exploring Some More" to extend the program. Do be sure to include "Saying Goodbye" to wrap things up.

Message:

Each program focuses on sharing Christian love in the world around us, from the dinner table to a church fellowship event, to a mission project, to a nature study, to a Christmas celebration. The message is woven through all of the program's activities.

Verse:

Children's Church is grounded in Scripture. Beloved Bible verses, stories, and poetry from the Psalms are the basis for the programs.

Opening:

The message of the program is revealed each week by eye-catching objects that are tucked into an envelope, a gift bag, a Bible, a hand, a shoebox house, a newspaper, or a gift box.

Sharing a Story:

Most of the stories are actively shared experiences since the kids participate in the telling. Motions, choral responses, question and answer, costumes, and paper creations invite them to jump into the story. On other occasions, toy animals, singing, and props make the story meaningful and memorable.

Praying:

The prayer that follows each story reflects the message of the day. While some prayers are traditional, others involve the kids more actively.

Exploring:

Through crafts, drama, adventures, art, games, object hunts, and songs, kids explore and experience the meaning of the Bible story and message. The activities are creative but not difficult. Care has been taken to use inexpensive and commonly available supplies. A helper is always a good idea, especially if the kids are very young or the group is large.

Snacking:

The snack ideas are easy for you and a treat for the kids. Each suggested snack is linked to the story and message to encourage continued discussion and smiling faces.

Exploring Some More:

Use these additional activities to extend the program or in place of the activity listed in "Exploring."

Saying Goodbye:

This is the time for the kids to gather up their crafts or keepsakes. Just before they leave, send them off with parting words to close the program and reinforce the message.

Thank you for sharing your love with the kids at your church or preschool. We hope you find this book a pleasure to use, kid-friendly, and fun. We wrote it just for you!

Lisa Flinn and Barbara Younger
Hillsborough, North Carolina

6

FAMILIES CAN PRAY

Opening a Letter:

Introduce the message by presenting a letter to the children. On a piece of stationery or plain paper, write: "Dear Grandma, Our family is worried. I think we should pray. Love, ME." Fold the letter and place it in an envelope.

Gather the children together. Hold up the envelope. If you have readers, choose a child to open and read the letter. If not, have a child open the envelope and then read the letter to the children yourself.

Ask: What do you think happened to make this family feel worried? (*Their dog is lost. The car isn't working. Their mother is sick.*)

Say: All families have problems and troubles. These problems and troubles can make families worry. Sometimes, we feel those worries right here, in our hearts. (*Place a hand over your heart.*) Jesus knows how we feel in our hearts. Jesus tells us, "Do not let your hearts be troubled. Believe in God, believe also in me" (John 14:1). Jesus wants us to pray to God and take our troubles to God when we are worried or scared.

Sharing a Story:

Children will respond to the story by displaying hand-drawn worried faces and decorated hearts. You will need supplies. Before children's church, make a sample to show the children. Draw a worried face on the front of the paper plate. Cut out a paper heart small enough to fit on the back of the plate. Color some simple decorations on the heart. Glue the heart to the back of the plate. Cut a paper heart for each child.

Start the story with a warm-up and an explanation of how the worried faces will be used.

Ask: Does this look like a worried face? (*Make a smiling face.*) (*No!*) Does this look like a worried face? (*Frown and wrinkle your brow.*) (*Yes!*)

Say: Our faces often show what we are feeling in our hearts. In today's story, a family is worried. Show me what their worried faces look like. (*Encourage everyone to look worried.*) Now we'll draw worried faces.

Give each child a paper plate, and set out the crayons. Show the children your sample. Have them draw a worried face on the front of the plate. Next, give everyone a heart to decorate. Have the children glue the heart to the back of the plate.

Explain that as you tell the story, they will follow your lead by looking at their drawing of a worried face, *saying: "Do not let your hearts be troubled,"* and then turning the plate to see their decorated heart.

Message:
Families can pray when they have cares and worries.

Bible Verse:
"Do not let your hearts be troubled. Believe in God, believe also in me." (John 14:1)

Supplies:
(for Opening a Letter)

sheet of paper

marker

envelope

Supplies:
(for Sharing a Story)

plain paper plates

light colored paper

scissors

crayons

glue

7

Tell the Story:

On a cloudy winter morning, a family woke up and found their house was very cold. Their mother said, "Oh no! Our furnace must be broken. This will cost a lot of money! And who knows when it can be fixed." She made a worried face. (Lead the children in looking at their worried face, *while saying the verse: "Do not let your hearts be troubled,"* and then turning the face over to see the heart.)

Shivering in his bathrobe, the father looked outside. "And now it's snowing! How will I get to work today? The snow is deep." He made a worried face. (Repeat same actions as above: look at face, say verse, look at heart.)

The mother said a prayer and then called the furnace repair shop. The father said a prayer and then shoveled the driveway. The kids put on their warmest clothes to play in the snow. They weren't worried at all until one of them slipped on the steps and cut his forehead. "He's bleeding!" shouted his sister. Now the kids looked worried. They said a prayer, too. (look at face, say verse, look at heart)

Just then, their next-door neighbor called out to them, "I'm a nurse. I can help! Come on over." The father and the kids hopped through the snow into Mrs. Smiley's warm house. She said, "You all look worried." (look at face, say verse, look at heart)

As the nurse fixed the brother's cut, a snowplow cleared the street. The father was glad. Soon at the family's cold house, the mother welcomed the furnace repairman. After he worked on the broken furnace, he said, "Lady, don't look so worried. The new part won't cost much, and your house will be warm soon." (look at face, say verse, look at heart)

The mother laughed with happiness. That night at dinner, the family talked about their worries. In their mealtime prayer, they thanked God for all the help they had been given. The mother said, "Not all of our worries go away so quickly or easily, but God is always with us." The father said, "And God knows how we feel when we are worried." The kids said, "Do not let your hearts be troubled. Believe in God!" (look at face, say verse, look at heart) **The End.**

Praying About Our Cares:

Have the children put their hands on their hearts. Pray the prayer.

Exploring Our Cares:

Children will personalize their own packs of Trouble Tissues. You will need small, travel-size packs of tissues (one per child) and stickers. Try to use heart stickers or stickers with a Christian theme.

To begin, give each child a pack of tissues, and set out the stickers. Invite the children to decorate their tissue packs.

Ask: Why do we need tissues? (*To blow our noses. To wipe our eyes. To cover a sneeze.*) Why might we wipe our eyes? (*Because we have allergies. Because we have been crying.*) Why do people cry? (*Because they are sad, angry, or worried.*)

Say: People cry sometimes when they are happy, but usually it means they have troubles. I cried when (*give an example*).

Ask: Can any of you remember a time when you cried? (*When my kitty died. When my tooth hurt. When my dad got mad at me.*)

Say: When you have worries and you cry, pray to God for help and use a Trouble Tissue to dry your eyes!

Snacking With Hearts:

Here are some snack ideas with a heart theme:

1) Draw large hearts on paper plates. Serve a snack of your choice on the hearts.

2) Use a heart-shaped cookie cutter to cut hearts from slices of bread (top with jelly) or from cheese slices (top with crackers). (Use the remainder of the bread to make croutons, or toss the extra cheese into a salad.)

3) Decorate packaged fruit or pudding cups with heart stickers.

As the children enjoy the snack, talk about ways they can show love to worried family members.

Exploring Some More:

Children will have fun playing a Bible verse circle game. Have them form a wide circle. You will need a paper heart.

Explain that everyone will *repeat: Do not let your hearts be troubled—* as one child, holding a paper heart, leaves his or her spot to run around the outside of the circle. That child, the Runner, drops a paper heart behind someone. The Runner slips into this place as the new Runner picks up the heart. Everyone *repeats, Do not let your hearts be troubled* again as the new Runner runs around the circle and drops the heart behind someone else.

Choose a child to start, and begin the game. If you are concerned about running, children can be asked to walk.

Saying Goodbye:

Invite the children to pick up their decorated paper plates from the story and their Trouble Tissues.

Say: Every family has worries. If you have a big worry in your heart, pray to God, but also tell a parent, teacher, or someone at church. And remember to share God's love in your family this week. Goodbye, Good Hearts!

Snack:
paper plates
snack of your
choice such as:
slices of bread
jelly
cheese slices
crackers
and heart-shaped
cookie cutter
fruit cups
pudding cups
heart stickers

Supplies:
(for Explore
Some More)
paper heart

...

Message:

Families try to please God.

Bible Verse:

"So whether we are at home or away, we make it our aim to please him." (2 Corinthians 5:9)

Supplies:

(for Opening a Letter)

sheet of paper

marker

envelope

FAMILIES AT HOME

Opening a Letter:

Introduce the message by presenting the children with a letter. To prepare, draw a simple house on a sheet of paper: use a square for the base, topped by an A-line roof, and finished with a door inside the square. On the paper write: "I drew this picture of my home. I live here with my family. We try to please God in what we say and do. Love, ME." Place the letter in an envelope.

Gather the children together. Hold up the envelope. If there are readers, choose one to open and read the letter; if not, open it and read the letter to the children yourself.

Say: When we please someone, we do things that will make the person happy.

Ask: Think of a time you tried to please someone in your family. (*I made a gift.*)

Say: It's good for everyone in a family to try to help each other be happy. It's also important for a family to try to please God.

Sharing a Story:

The children will pretend to be a family as you lead them in the actions. Begin the story with everyone seated.

Say: Let's pretend we are a family! I will be your parent, and you will be my children. We'll imagine we're at home. As I tell the story, you will copy my actions.

Tell the Story:

Our family is at home on a Saturday morning. I say, "Wake up, sleepy heads!" (yawn, covering mouth with hand) **It's time to smile and thank God for this new day.** (stretch arms above head) **God is pleased to see our family rise and shine!**

Now let's get dressed and start this wonderful day. (pretend to pull t-shirt over head) **Let's eat breakfast.** (pretend to spoon from cupped hand to mouth) **Please pass the milk, and please pass the cereal. We sit together at the table. God is pleased that our family is being kind to one another.**

I say, "Kids, our neighbor needs our help this morning." We'll take her some bread (extend palm), **we'll walk her dogs** (stand, extend closed fist downward as if holding leash), **and we'll take in her newspaper** (stoop, extend hand down and grab). **God is pleased when our family shows love and care for our neighbor.**

At lunch we say, "God is love. God is good. Now we thank God for our food." (fold hands in prayer) **God is pleased when we remember to be thankful. After lunch, I read a Bible story to you.** (touch palms together to be a book) **We please God when we read the Bible because it tells us important things to know for living good lives.**

In the afternoon, we work together to put clean sheets on the beds. (extend arms, pull back) **Next, we play a funny game as we match the socks in the laundry basket!** (grin, put hands to cheeks) **When we work together in our homes, we please God.**

Now, we bake muffins to take to church on Sunday morning. (pretend to stir ingredients in a bowl) **We please God when we make the church family our family.**

Then we make Silly Soup with the leftover food in the refrigerator. You say, "May we ask friends to come over and eat?" I say, "Yes!" **We please God when we welcome people into our homes.**

Finally, it's time for bed. We wash our hands (rub hands together), **brush our teeth** (use forefinger like a brush), **and say our prayers** (fold hands). **We pray for our family and friends. We talk to God about everything. God is pleased when we pray.**

10

Praying About Pleasing God:

Have the children form a circle. Ask them to hold hands and prayer the prayer.

Say: Let us pray a prayer about pleasing God.

Exploring:

The children will make House Door Hangers. Before Children's Church, cut and assemble the House Door Hangers, one per child and one as a sample. Cut sheets of construction paper in half lengthwise. These rectangles are the front of the houses. Cut triangular roof pieces, one per house.

Glue a roof onto the front of each house. On the roof, print: "Please God." Cut lengths of yarn or ribbon about ten inches long and staple it in a loop to the roof.

Finish the sample by drawing windows and a door on one of the houses.

Show the house to the children. Read the message and demonstrate how it works.

Say: In our story, we heard many ways that a family can please God at home.

Ask: Can you remember how the family pleased God? (*being kind, helping the neighbor, working together, reading Bible stories, praying, welcoming friends*)

Say: We want to please God at home. Your Door Hanger will help you remember!

Give each child a door hanger, and set out the crayons. Invite them to draw windows and a door on their houses.

Snacking:

Cut cheese slices in half from corner to corner to make triangles. On a platter, arrange cracker squares topped with triangle cheese roofs.

As children eat, ask them to tell their favorite ways to please God at home.

Exploring Some More:

Take children on a pretend Pleasing God House Tour. Move to a new space, or have the children follow you around the room, or walk in place as you point out the imaginary houses. Encourage them to picture the home you are describing. Explain that in all of these types of homes, there are families who try to please God.

Say: Here are some homes in the big city. Look at that tall apartment building.

Down the street, a family makes their home above their grocery store.

On the corner there is a shelter for families who don't have homes of their own.

Now we're in the neighborhoods outside the city. Here is a mobile home park with lots of shade trees and white fences. Thirty families live here.

Along the next street, we see many different houses in many colors and sizes.

Near the shopping mall is a street of townhouses that look like our door hangers.

Out in the country, we see a farmhouse, then a log cabin, then a lake house.

Families in all of these homes try their best to please God.

Have the children draw a picture of one of the pretend homes they saw on the tour.

Saying Goodbye:

Have the children hold their House Door Hanger. Ask them to *say together: Families please God at home.*

Say: When you go home, hang your paper house over a doorknob. Tell your family that it is important to find ways to please God every day. Share God's love in your family by being kind, enthusiastic, and considerate. Goodbye, Family Kids!

Prayer of Pleasing:

God of Love, whether we are at home or away, we make it our aim to please you. Help us to do our best! Amen.

Supplies:

(for Exploring)

light-colored construction paper

crayons

glue

scissors

tape or stapler

yarn or ribbon

Snack:

square crackers

single slices of American cheese

Supplies:

(for Exploring Some More)

paper

crayons or markers

Message:
Families can have fun.

Bible Verse:
"He will yet fill your mouth with laughter, and your lips with shouts of joy." (Job 8:21)

Supplies:
(for Opening a Letter)
postcard
pen or marker

Supplies:
(for Tell the Story)
basket, bag, or box
DVD/videotape
children's book
rubber spatula
birthday item
ball
garden tool
holiday item
road map
Bible

Opening a Letter:

Introduce today's message by sharing a postcard with the children. To prepare, use a postcard sent to you, purchase one, or make your own by gluing a magazine photo on an index card. On the message portion of the postcard, print: "Our family is having fun! Wish you were here!" If using a postcard you received, tape a piece of paper over the original message and then print your own.

Gather the children together. Hold up the postcard. If you have readers, choose a child to read the postcard, or read it to the children and then pass it around.

Ask: Why do you think this family is having fun? (*They're on vacation.*)

Say: People often send postcards to show the places they are visiting and to tell you that they are having a good time. God is glad when families have fun together.

Sharing a Story:

This story tells different ways that families have fun. You'll need the objects in the supplies list. Place the items in a bag, box, or basket.

Tell the Story:

Here is a story about the life of the Fun Family. Listen for clues to their fun.

(Show basket) **What's this?** This is a basket of food the family is sharing on a picnic. After eating, they take a hike in the woods and then go swimming. Have you ever been on a picnic with your family?

(Show DVD or videotape) **What's this?** On Sunday night the family is tired. They decide to watch a movie together. They laugh and laugh. What fun! Have you ever watched a funny movie with your family?

(Show children's book) **What's this?** On Monday, they visit the library and check out books. At home they read the books. Have you ever read a book with your family?

(rubber spatula) **What's this?** On Tuesday, the family uses a rubber spatula to frost a birthday cake. They giggle. What fun! Have you ever gotten ready for a party?

(birthday item) **What's this?** The family sings and laughs as they celebrate sister's birthday. What fun! Have you ever celebrated a birthday with your family?

(ball) **What's this?** On Wednesday, the family watches a game at school. They cheer for the team then go home and play a ball game. Have you ever played ball with your family?

(garden tool) **What's this?** On Thursday, they plant flowers and clean their yard. They like working together. What fun! Do you ever work with your family?

(holiday item) **What's this?** On Friday, the family starts planning for the holiday. They go shopping for a few things. What fun! Do you ever celebrate holidays with your family?

(road map) **What's this?** On Saturday, the family looks at a map to find their way to a park. It's a beautiful day to be together outdoors. What fun! Do you ever visit parks with your family?

(Bible) **What's this?** On Saturday night, the family reads stories from the Bible. What fun! Do you ever read Bible stories with your family?

That's the story of seven days of family fun with the Fun Family. And it sounds like you have fun with your families, too!

12

Praying About Fun:

Open the Bible you used during the story to Job 8:21. Read the verse. If practical, have the children reach in and touch the Bible while you pray the Prayer About Fun.

Exploring:

Lead the children in a song, using the objects from the story. The song is set to the tune of "This is the Way We Wash Our Clothes." As you begin each verse, pick up the appropriate object and send it around the circle. You may sing the verse as many times as needed to send the object completely around the circle.

Sing:

Basket: This is the way we go on a picnic, go on a picnic, go on a picnic.
This is the way we go on a picnic, having fun with our families.

DVD/videotape: This is the way we watch a movie...

Children's book: This is the way we read good books...

Rubber spatula: This is the way we frost a cake...

Birthday item: This is the way we have a party...

Ball: This is the way we play a sport...

Garden tool: This is the way we garden together...

Holiday item: This is the way we celebrate...

Road map: This is the way we go on a trip...

Bible: This is the way we read the Bible...

Next, have the children each tell a way that their family has fun together.

Say: Families have fun doing special things together such as taking trips or having a parties, but families can have fun as they do their everyday activities, too.

Ask: What are some of the chores and activities your family does every day at home? *(set the table, pick up toys, watch television)*

Say: One way to keep these everyday activities fun is by not acting grumpy and by not fussing and fighting with one another. Put on a smiling face! God is glad when families have fun together.

Snacking With a Basket:

Put today's snack in a basket, and take the children on a picnic.

Exploring Some More:

Celebrate family fun with Family Fun Postcards. Before Children's Church, print: "He will yet fill your mouth with laughter" (Job 8:21) on one side of each index card.

Give out the index cards. Have the children turn the card to the blank side. Invite them to draw a picture of their families. When the children are finished, ask them to describe their drawings. Next, say the Bible verse with the children.

If you have brought stickers, have the children put a sticker on the side of the card with the Bible verse. Suggest they give their postcard to a family member.

Saying Goodbye:

Say: When you are at home today, talk with your family about some of the activities you enjoy doing together. Make a plan to do some of those activities soon, maybe even today. Remember to share God's love in your family with laughter. Goodbye, Funny Bones!

Sharing God's Love in Our Family

**Bible
Verse:**

"Be kind to one
another,
tenderhearted,
forgiving one
another,
as God in Christ
has forgiven you."
(Ephesians 4:32)

Supplies:

(for Opening a
Letter)

piece of stationery
or paper

or an "I'm sorry"
greeting card

pen or marker

envelope

Supplies:

(for Sharing a Story
and Tell the Story)

a paper heart for
every child

scissors

construction paper

FAMILIES FORGIVE

Opening a Letter:

To introduce the message, present a letter to the children. Prepare by buying a greeting card that asks for forgiveness, or by printing a letter on a piece of stationery or paper. On the card or letter, print: "Dear Mom, I'm sorry I broke the lamp and blamed it on someone else. Love, ME." Place the card or letter in an envelope.

Gather the children together. Hold up the envelope. If you have readers, choose a child to open and read the card or letter aloud. If not, invite a child to open the envelope, and read the card or letter to the children yourself.

Say: People aren't perfect. Both grownups and kids make mistakes that hurt others.

Ask: Have you ever accidentally hurt another person by what you have said or done? How? (*knocked my cousin down, broke my brother's toy*)

Say: Even when we hurt someone by accident, it's important to say we're sorry.

Ask: Have you ever been angry at someone and then hurt that person? How? (*by saying mean things, telling a lie, hitting*) Has someone ever been mean to you? How did it feel? (*I was upset. I cried. I was sad.*)

Say: Families can hurt each other from time to time. And when those times come, the family needs to talk about the problem. After working out the problem, a family must try to forgive one another. The Bible tells us: "Be kind to one another, tender-hearted, forgiving one another as God in Christ has forgiven you" (Ephesians 4:32).

Sharing a Story:

Taken from Luke 10:38-42, this embellished story tells of anger and forgiveness. Martha is angry with her sister Mary during a visit from Jesus. In response to the story, children will open and close a paper heart. They will open the heart when Martha is happy and close the heart when Martha is angry.

To prepare, cut a heart for each child. Take a sheet of construction paper, fold it in half horizontally; then into quarters, then into eighths. Open the sheet and cut along the fold lines to yield eight pieces. Fold each piece in half and snip a heart. Begin cutting at the folded edge. Repeat until you have a heart for each child and one for yourself.

Say: This is a story of two sisters who lived in Bible days. Martha may be the older sister because she appears to be charge of their home. Mary doesn't seem to mind that Martha is in charge because Mary is interested in other things. During the story, we will learn how Martha, the older sister, feels as we watch her open her heart with happiness or close her heart in anger.

Give each child a paper heart. Use a heart yourself to cue the children.

Tell the Story:

As I tell the story, watch what I do with my paper heart. Then you do the same!

One day while Mary was reading a scroll and Martha was sweeping the floor, someone knocked on their door. Martha opened the door to find their dear friend Jesus on the step.

"Jesus!" she said. "How wonderful to see you! Welcome. Come in." Martha's heart opened with gladness. (hold up opened heart)

Jesus came inside. Mary hurried to greet him. Jesus was dusty, thirsty, and hungry. Martha went out for a bucket of water. She asked Mary to bring towels. Jesus washed his face and hands. Then the sisters washed and dried his feet.

Martha asked Mary to come and help her carry out some cups. Martha put the cups on a tray and wondered, "Where's Mary?" She found cool jugs of water and wondered again, "Where's Mary?" When she took the cups and jugs to the room where Jesus was, her heart closed in anger. (fold heart closed) **Mary was listening to Jesus!**

Martha decided not to be angry. Her heart opened. (open heart) **She washed the grapes and cut the cheese. "Mary!" she called out. Martha filled a basket with bread and a bowl with nuts. "Mary!" she called again. When Martha carried the snack into the room, Mary was sitting at the feet of Jesus, listening to a story. Martha's heart closed with anger toward her sister.** (fold heart closed)

Martha banged the pots and pans and stamped around as she heated some lentil stew. Then she remembered how much she liked to hear Jesus' stories. She smiled and her heart opened a little. (open heart a bit) **Finally the stew was ready. Martha brought out the big, warm bowl.**

She set the bowl down and said,"Jesus, don't you care that my sister hasn't helped me at all?" Martha realized she felt angry at Jesus, too. Her heart closed. (fold heart)

"Martha, Martha," Jesus said. "You worry about so many things. Your sister Mary chose the better part of my visit. No one can take away this time we spent together."

Martha's heart trembled. (shake hearts) **She knew that by working so hard, she had missed a lot of Jesus' visit. Maybe she didn't need to prepare so much food. Martha wanted to be a good hostess, but a good hostess wouldn't leave her guests. Jesus was right. Her heart opened a bit.** (open heart a bit) **She said,"I'm sorry, Mary."** (open heart a bit more) **Mary answered,"I forgive you, sister. I should have been more helpful. Martha's heart opened wide with love.** (open heart) **Families forgive.**

Praying About Forgiveness:

Have the children hold their paper heart so they can open and close it during the prayer. Pray the Forgiveness Prayer.

Exploring:

Children will make Forgiveness Cards. See supplies for what you will need.

Fold each sheet of paper in half to form a card. Go to each child, open up the card, and trace her or his hand on the inside of the card. Next, invite the children to glue their paper hearts onto the palms of their traced hands. Have them sign their names and then fold the card closed with their hand and name on the inside.

Have those who can, print: "I'm Sorry!" on the outside of the card. (Assist children who cannot write yet.) Invite the children to decorate around the words.

Say: **Give this card to someone in your family the next time you've done something wrong, and you want to apologize. God wants us to ask for forgiveness when we have hurt someone, and God wants families to be tenderhearted and forgiving.**

Snacking With Cake:

Introduce children to the old tradition of Forgiveness Cake. Years ago, when forgiveness was needed, two people shared a small cake.

After explaining this tradition, group children in pairs. Give each pair a snack cake or muffin to share. Provide a plastic knife or butter knife and napkins. Invite each pair to slice their cake in two. As they each enjoy their half, encourage them to talk about people they may need to forgive.

Forgiveness Prayer:

God of Love,
when our hearts
feel closed
(close heart)
because we
are angry,
help us to say we
are sorry so our
hearts can open
again in love.
(open heart)
When our hearts
feel closed
(close heart)
because we
feel hurt,
help us to
forgive so our
hearts can open
again in love.
(open heart)
Amen.

Supplies:

(for Exploring)

sheet of paper
(1 per child)

paper heart
(1 per child)

glue

markers

Snack:

snack cakes or
muffins

plastic knifes or
butter knifes

napkins

Exploring Some More:

Have children practice saying "I'm sorry" with two simple action games.

Sorry Train:

You will lead the first round as the "Engine." Have the children line up behind you. Ask them to hook onto the Engine by grasping the right elbow of the child in front of them. Have everyone pump their left arm and begin to move slowly around the room. **Say** (*in chug-a-lug style*): **I'm so sorry. I'm so sorry. I'm so sorry. I'm so sorry, forgive me-ee-.** Let each child take a turn as the Engine.

Sorry Circle:

This is played like "Ring Around the Rosy," except with the new words: "I'm so sorry that I hurt you. I didn't really mean to. Forgive me, forgive me. Families Forgive!" Have the children hold hands as they move in a circle. At the last line, have everyone drop hands and cross their arms across their chests.

Play several times, moving the circle in opposite directions.

Saying Goodbye:

Have the children hold their Forgiveness Card.

Say: Don't forget to give someone in your family your Forgiveness Card the next time you want to ask for forgiveness. What a wonderful way to say you are sorry. In all families, people make mistakes. And in all families, people need forgiving. Let's say the Bible verse together.

Lead children in saying the Bible verse: **"Be kind to one another, tenderhearted, forgiving one another as God in Christ has forgiven you"** (Ephesians 4:32).

Say: Forgiving one another is one way to share God's love in you family. Goodbye, Forgiving Kids!

HAPPY MEALTIMES

Opening a Letter:

Introduce the message by sharing a letter with the children. To prepare, find a magazine or newspaper picture of one of these:

1) a dining table;
2) a place setting;
3) a serving dish filled with food.

Glue your selection to a piece of paper. On the paper, print the sentence that corresponds with your picture choice: "Dear Friend, This is 1) where my family eats supper; 2) the kind of dishes we use; 3)one of my favorite foods. Bye, ME." Fold the letter and place it in an envelope.

Gather the children together. Hold up the envelope. If you have readers, choose a child to open and read the letter aloud. If there are no readers, invite a child to open the envelope, and then read the letter to the children yourself.

Say: The child who wrote this is thinking about mealtime and must be hungry!

Ask: When you're hungry, what foods are your favorites? (*pizza, a peanut butter and jelly sandwich, spaghetti and meatballs*)

Say: We eat breakfast, lunch, and dinner because our bodies need food. When we have a happy mealtime with our families, we also feed our hearts with love and happiness. One way families share God's love is by enjoying their meals together.

Sharing a Story:

Certain practices contribute to a happy mealtime! Today's story describes these. You will lead the children in singing responses, which are set to the tune of "If You're Happy and You Know It."

Say: You're going to hear a story that describes ways to enjoy a meal with your family. I will first talk about one of the ways, and then we'll sing about it together.

Tell the story:

Suppertime is coming! Let's have a happy mealtime together! First, you'll help set the table, putting out plates and cups, knives and forks, spoons and napkins. The table is ready for supper now.

Sing: If you're happy and you know it, set the table.
If you're happy and you know it, set the table.
If you're happy and you know it, then happy mealtimes show it.
If you're happy and you know it, set the table.

Next, you'll help to fix the meal. There is so much to be done in the kitchen! You stir and shake; you sprinkle and spread. The food smells wonderful, doesn't it?

Sing: If you're happy and you know it, fix the food.
If you're happy and you know it, fix the food.
If you're happy and you know it, then happy mealtimes show it.
If you're happy and you know it, fix the food.

"Hey, everyone! Supper is ready." The family sits down around the table. Then you all bow your heads for prayer: "Thank you for the world so sweet. Thank you for the food we eat. Thank you for the birds that sing. Thank you, God, for everything. Amen." After the prayer, everyone smiles.

Sharing God's Love in Our Family

Bible Verse:
"So, whether you eat or drink, or whatever you do, do everything for the glory of God." (1 Corinthians: 10:31)

Supplies:
(for Opening a Letter)

pictures from a magazine or newspaper

paper

envelope

glue

Supplies:
(for Tell the Story)

plates

cups

knives

forks

spoons

napkins

17

Supplies:
(for Exploring)

disposable
8oz. cups
(1 for each child)

drinking straws
(3 for each child)

a lump of
play clay
(see recipe, p. 19)

a half or whole
sheet of round
label stickers for
each child, plus
extras for teacher
(may be purchased
where office
supplies are sold)

fine-tip markers
or pens

fluted-edge, round
coffee filters
(3 for each child)

clear, adhesive tape

Mealtime Prayer:
God of Love,
we are thankful
for our families,
for food we share,
and for the love
that fills
our hearts with
happiness.
Amen.

18

Sing: If you're happy and you know, say a prayer.
If you're happy and you know it, say a prayer.
If you're happy and you know it, then happy mealtimes show it.
If you're happy and you know it, say a prayer.

The family puts their napkins on their laps. They say, "Please pass this" and "Please pass that" and "Thank you" every time.

Sing: If you're happy and you know it, be polite.
If you're happy and you know it, be polite.
If you're happy and you know it, then happy mealtimes show it.
If you're happy and you know it, be polite.

"Mmm," everyone says, "this meal is really good!" The family tastes every bite. No one gobbles the food. Instead, the family talks and laughs all during supper.

Sing: If you're happy and you know it, enjoy the meal.
If you're happy and you know it, enjoy the meal.
If you're happy and you know, then happy mealtimes show it.
If you're happy and you know it, enjoy the meal.

The mealtime is over. Tummies are full of food and hearts are full of happiness.

Sing: If you're happy and you know it, show your love.
If you're happy and you know it, show your love.
If you're happy and you know, then happy mealtimes show it.
If you're happy and you know it, show your love.

Because families are very busy, they sometimes feel tired and grumpy at suppertime.

Ask: Can you think of some ways you can help make mealtime happy? (*don't tease my sister, try new foods, don't make a mess*)

We can have happy mealtimes if we remember to share God's love with our families.

Praying At Mealtime:

Have the children place one hand over their heart and one hand over their tummy. Pray the Mealtime Prayer.

Exploring:

Children will make Fancy Flower Pot Centerpieces to decorate their family tables. See Supplies for what will be needed.

Before Children's Church, use a marker to print 1 Corinthians 10:31 on enough round stickers so that each child can have one.

Begin by giving the children stickers and markers or pens. Have them draw smiley faces on their stickers. As they draw, place one of the "1 Corinthians 10:31" stickers on a cup for each child. When the children are finished creating smiley faces, give them each a cup. Invite them to decorate the cups with the smiley stickers.

Next, give each child a piece of play clay to put in the bottom of the cup. This clay will help weight the cup and anchor the drinking straws.

Help the children make three flowers each, using the coffee filters and straws. Have them fold a filter in half and then in half again. Demonstrate how to pinch the pointed end and roll it between their fingers. Poke this tapered end into a straw. Secure with tape. Repeat until all the flowers are finished.

Complete the centerpieces by gently pushing the flower stem straws into the clay in the cup. Use a marker or pen to print each child's initials on the bottom of the cup.

Say: You made Fancy Flower Pot Centerpieces that are perfect for your tables at home. They are decorated with reminders to have happy mealtimes with your family.

The smiling faces remind us to smile. The sticker with writing on it is a reference to the Bible verse for today. (Say the verse.) **Your parents can use their Bibles to look up the verse at home.**

Snacking With Tableware:

Serve any snack you like, but make it special by giving each child a place setting. Use real dishes and flatware, or pretty paper plates and cups with plastic utensils. Don't forget cloth or paper napkins. Place the snack items on serving plates.

Encourage the children to practice saying, "Please pass" and "Thank you." Make happy conversation and enjoy!

Exploring Some More:

Have the children practice a table grace and then create Play Clay Fruits and Vegetables. If you want to send the fruits and vegetables home with the children, purchase the clay or make your own.

Begin by saying the prayer used in the story. Next invite the children to *say it with you, line by line:*

> *Thank you for the world so sweet.*
> *Thank you for the food we eat.*
> *Thank you for the birds that sing.*
> *Thank you God for everything. Amen.*

Lead the children in saying the prayer. Ask if anyone can say the whole prayer.

Next, bring out the play clay. Challenge the children to make fruits and vegetables. If you want to send the fruits and vegetables home with the children, have them put their creations on a paper plate.

Saying Goodbye:

Have the children hold their Fancy Flower Pot Centerpieces. Lead them in saying the Bible verse one more time.

Say: With your smiling faces and happy hearts, help your family to enjoy mealtimes. That's a great way to share God's love in your family. Goodbye, Diners!

If you have decided to do so, send the Play Clay Fruits and Vegetables home with the children.

Recipe:

1 cup flour

1/2 cup salt

2 tsp. cream of tartar

food coloring

1 Tbsp. of vegetable oil

1 cup water

Mix the dry ingredients. Add food coloring, oil, and water. Cook over medium heat for several minutes. Let cool, then knead. Play clay stores well in airtight containers.

Snacking:

snack of your choice

Prepare a table-setting with:

real dishes and flatware (or pretty paper plates, cups) napkins

serving dishes

Supplies:

(for Exploring Some More)

play clay in several colors

paper plates

19

PLEASANT UNITY

Message:

Families should live in peace and unity.

Bible Verse:

"How very good and pleasant it is when kindred live together in unity!" (Psalm 133:1)

Supplies:

(for Opening a Letter)

2 pieces of stationery or paper

pen or marker

two envelopes

Opening a Letter:

Introduce the message by sharing two different letters with the children.

First letter: "Dear Dad, The Bible says it is good when kindred live together in unity. I don't know what two of the words mean: *kindred* and *unity*. Love, ME."

Second letter: "My dear child, The word *kindred* means "family." The word *unity* means "joined together." The Bible is saying how pleasant it is when families are joined together in love and peace. Love, Dad."

Place each letter in an envelope. Mark the first letter "#1" and the second letter "#2."

Gather the children together. Hold up envelope #1 for all to see. If you have readers, choose a child to open and read the letter aloud. If there are no readers, invite a child to open the envelope, and then read the letter yourself. Next, bring out the second envelope and do the same.

Ask: How does it feel when the people in your family are joined together in love, and no one is fussing? (*good, happy, nice to be home*) Does it feel different when the family is fussing and fighting? (*Yes, sad, angry. I want to be alone.*)

Say: Most families want to live together in peace and unity. One way that we can share God's love in our families is by being peaceful and pleasant.

Sharing a Story:

Children will meet the Fussing Family and the Favorite Family to understand how they are different. The story follows the pattern of "Going on a Bear Hunt." Ask the children to repeat each line after you. As you tell the story and as they repeat each line, pat palms of hands on thighs to imitate footsteps: right-left, right-left.

Tell the Story:

Come with me as we meet the Fussing Family. After I say a line, you are to repeat that line. And make footsteps like this: (demonstrate: pat, pat, pat, pat.)

> They're going to the grocery store.
> Mom says, "Be good!"
> But kids crash down the aisles.
> And Mom starts yelling.
> They're fussing, and they're fighting.
>
> They're going to eat their supper.
> Dad is tired and grumpy.
> Someone says the wrong thing.
> Now they're fussing, and they're fighting.

Now follow me as we meet the Favorite Family:

> They're going to the grocery store.
> Mom says, "Be good!"
> The kids find the cereal.
> Mom thanks her helpers.
> They're smiling, and they're laughing.
>
> They're going to eat their supper.
> Dad is tired and grumpy.
> The kids tell silly jokes.
> Now they're smiling, and they're laughing.

20

Ask: Both families went to the store and ate supper, so what was different about them? (*One family was fussing; the other family was getting along.*)

Say: The Favorite Family joined together to be kind and helpful, even when there was a problem. No family is perfect. Most families have times when they fuss or fight. When your family gets upset, try to be kind and helpful to one another.

Praying About Family:

Have the children link arms with one another. Pray the Family Prayer.

Exploring:

The children will celebrate family unity by making Family Unity Chains. Before Children's Church, prepare the paper strips needed to make the chains. Select a variety of colors. Cut twelve strips (1- by 9-inches) from each sheet. One sheet per child.

Say: Earlier I explained that the word *unity* means "joined together." Our Bible verse tells us that it is good and pleasant when families live in *unity*. We're going to have a good time joining our family together with paper chains.

Ask: Has anyone made a paper chain before? (Let the children explain the process.)

Begin by having the children each select a paper strip. Have them use a marker or crayon to print the name of a parent on the strip. (Assist children who can't write yet.) Next, have the children glue their strip together to form a ring, with the name on the outside. Have the children create a strip for their other parent, and then strips for their other family members. Each time, have them glue the strip into a ring.

To form a chain, have the children join these rings together by looping new strips between the name rings. Finish by adding a loop at each end.

Have the children hold up their paper chains. *Ask them to repeat these words after you: My family is joined in unity.*

Snacking on Cereal:

To extend the fun with multicolored rings, serve a ring-shaped cereal. Give the children napkins to spread out in front of them. Serve them each a scoop of cereal. Invite them to create pretend chains and other designs with the cereal.

Exploring Some More:

Play a game of "Don't Break the Chain."

Before Children's Church, make a length of paper chain. During the game, the children will stand on either side of the chain and then grasp a ring. Following your instructions, the group will move together, as they try not to break the chain.

Say: Let's tiptoe, tiptoe, tiptoe down the hall,
Tiptoe quietly past our sleeping sister's room.
Let's march, march, march towards Mom,
And help her carry in the shopping bags.
Let's walk, walk, walk around the block. Walk with our family in unity.

If the chain is broken, you can mend it with tape or a stapler, **saying: Just like the Favorite Family, we want to stay happily joined together.** If time permits, let the children help you think of more paper chain adventures to add to the lyrics above.

Saying Goodbye:

Have the children pick up their individual Family Unity Chain.

Say: May each of your families be joined together in peace and unity. That's a great way to share God's love in the family! Goodbye, Family Peacemakers!

Sharing God's Love in Our Family

**Bible
Verse:**
"Train children in
the right way."
(Proverbs 22:6)

Supplies:
(for Opening
a Letter)

stationery or
paper

pen or marker

envelope

Supplies:
(for Sharing a
Story)

toy animal

PARENTS TEACH US

Opening a Letter:

Introduce the message by sharing a letter with the children. Prepare by printing the following letter on stationery or paper: "Dear Mom and Dad, I want to take off my training wheels. Love, ME." Place the letter in an envelope.

Gather the children together. Hold up the envelope. If you have readers, choose a child to open and read the letter. If not, have a child open the envelope, and then read the letter to the children yourself.

Ask: What are training wheels? (*Two extra wheels put on the rear wheels of a bike to keep it from tipping over.*) Why would a child want to take the wheels off? (*To learn to ride the bike without the wheels.*) Who might teach the child to ride without the training wheels? (*Mom or Dad, an older brother or sister*)

Say: The word *training* means "teaching." Training wheels help teach kids to ride their bikes. The Bible speaks to parents about training their children. It says, "Train children in the right way" (Proverbs 22:6). This means that parents are supposed to teach their children lots of things.

Ask: What is something your parents have trained or taught you to do? (*play a board game, tie my shoelaces, say a bedtime prayer*) Did your parents teach you the right way or the best way to do these things?

Say: Parents want their children to grow up to live good and happy lives. They teach their children many things.

Sharing a Story:

As they listen to the story, children will consider the things parents teach them at different ages. Bring in a toy animal to act as Tim or Tia, the story's narrator. Use a silly voice for the animal and move him/her about as you speak. Pause where indicated in the story and invite the children to respond.

Tell the story:

Hello, kids! My name is Tim/Tia Talk-a-lot and I'm seven years old. Guess what! I'm adopted! I'm happy to have parents. They teach me the right way to act. Do you have parents? (pause)

Some kids have adoptive parents who raise them. Others have foster parents, step-parents, regular parents, or grandparents who raise them. No matter what kind of parents we have, it's good they're here to teach us things we need to know.

When you were little, did your parents teach you how to button and zip? (pause) Drink from a cup? (pause) Brush your teeth? (pause)

Did they teach you how to show your love with big hugs? (pause) By saying, "I love you?" (pause) By praying at bedtime with the family? (pause)

Did they teach you the right ways to act with others by saying "Please" and "Thank you?" (pause) By sharing toys? (pause) And by being kind and generous? (pause)

Hey, I can remember when my parents taught me to eat! (Fill in whatever the toy animal would eat: fish, worms, honey, crumbs, bugs, etc.) Do you remember your parents teaching you how to how to hold a fork? (pause) Put your napkin in your lap? (pause) Chew your food carefully? (pause)

Now that you're bigger, have your parents taught you new things like how to tie your shoelaces? (pause) How to shampoo your hair? (pause) Hang up your towel? (pause)

Have you learned your colors? (pause) **Your numbers?** (pause) **Your ABC's?** (pause) **Are you learning to bounce a ball?** (pause) **Ride a bike?** (pause) **Swing all by yourself?** (pause)

Are your parents teaching you not to hit others? (pause) **To play fair?** (pause) **To be helpful?** (pause)

Hey! The last time I helped my mother I ended up making a big mess, but she loves me anyway. Your parents love you, too. That's why they want to teach you about God. **Do they read Bible stories to you?** (pause) **Talk to you about church?** (pause) **Pray with you?** (pause)

Parents want to teach you the right ways. Learning about God is especially important. Goodbye for now!

Praying About Learning:

Invite the children to repeat your words and motions. Pray the Prayer of Learning.

Exploring:

For this activity, the children will each take a turn talking to Tim or Tía Talks-a-lot. They will tell the animal something a parent is teaching them now or something they would like to learn. If a child has difficulty responding, use the animal's voice to prompt the child with questions: What about learning to whistle, snap fingers, throw a football, jump rope, do a cartwheel?

With a larger group, one round with the toy animal may be enough. If you have a smaller group, you can **pose a few more questions: What's something your parents could teach you to do outdoors? In the kitchen? At Christmas time? When you are a teenager?**

Snacking With a Parent:

Invite a parent with a sense of humor to join the children for snack time. Before Children's Church, make jelly and butter sandwich quarters, two per child.

The children will end up teaching the parent how to correctly make a jelly and butter sandwich. Ahead of time, explain to the parent that he or she is going to be invited to demonstrate how to make the sandwich. But the parent is to take silly steps such as putting the jar of jelly onto a slice of bread or turning the butter tub upside down and using it as a drum.

Place all of the items on the table, near the parent. Arrange the children so everyone can see. As the parent makes the sandwich, invite the children to call out what she or he is doing wrong. When the sandwich is finally made correctly, thank the parent.

Say: Sometimes kids can teach things to parents!

Let your parent guest enjoy the sandwich he or she created and serve the sandwich quarters to the children.

The Prayer of Learning:
God of Love, may I learn with my mind (*point to temple*) and my heart (*point to heart*) to do the right things with my words (*point to mouth*) and with my hands (*hold out hands.*) Amen.

Supplies:
(for Exploring)
a toy animal

Snack:
sandwich bread
jelly
tub of spreadable butter
butter knife
plate

Exploring Some More:

Teach the children a song about learning, set to the tune of "Three Blind Mice." Each verse repeats the same line for lines one, two, and six. Encourage the children to sing these along with you. You can sing lines three, four, and five by yourself.

Sing: We are children, we are children!
See how we learn, see how we learn.
We learn to button and drink from a cup,
To use the potty and play with the pup.
Can you see how fast we grow up?
We are children!

We are children, we are children!
See how we learn, see how we learn.
We count and color and write our names.
We learn our address and play new games.
Did you ever see such kids in your life?
We are children!

We are children, we are children!
See how we learn, see how we learn.
We learn to swing, to bike, to skate,
We learn to be kind and not to hate.
Did you ever see such kids in your life?
We are children!

We are children, we are children!
See how we learn, see how we learn.
We learn of the Bible and God who loves us.
We're taught to love and how to behave.
Do you know we heard the examples you gave?
We are children!

Sing the song another round or two, as time permits.

Saying Goodbye:

Invite the children to close their eyes and picture the face of someone in their family who takes care of them. Then ask them to open their eyes again. **Say: God wants parents to teach their children the right ways. And God wants you to learn the right things. One way we can share God's love in the family is by listening and learning. Goodbye, Listeners and Learners!**

24

LOVING FRIENDS

Opening a Gift Bag:

To introduce the message, tuck a clock or a watch into a gift bag.

Gather the children together. Hold up the gift bag.

Say: I wonder what's in this gift bag. Here's a hint: I wonder what time it is, too.

Ask: What do you think is in the gift bag? (*a clock, a watch*)

Say: You're right! It's a clock/watch.

Read the time for the children.

Say: There's a verse in the Bible that says, "A friend loves at all times" (Proverbs 17:17). So whatever time it is, that's a good time to show love to your friends.

Ask: What do you think it means to love a friend at all times? (*You don't get mad and walk away. You are kind to your friend. You don't ignore your friend. You love your friend even when he or she is being mean.*)

Say: God wants us to love our friends even when we are angry at them, even when we are busy, even when we are tired, and even when we would rather not play with them. A good friend loves at all times, even when times are rough or difficult.

Sharing a Story:

The following story gives examples of times when a friend is loving and times when a friend is not. Ask the children to respond to the question, "Loving friend?" with a thumbs up for "yes" and a thumbs down for "no." Practice this a few times and begin.

Tell the Story:

Jackson and Matt were really good friends. One day, Jackson's mom invited Matt to go to the zoo with them.

"Guess what?" Jackson said when he called up Matt, "You get to come to the zoo with me. I can't wait. You're my good friend, and we have fun together."

Loving friend? (thumbs up)

Getting into the car, Matt stepped on one of Jackson's plastic cars. "You broke it!" Jackson shouted in a mean voice.

Loving friend? (thumbs down)

Jackson realized he had been mean. He shouldn't have left his toy car on the floor of the car. It wasn't Matt's fault that he stepped on it. "I'm sorry," he said to Matt.

Loving friend? (thumbs up)

Message:
Friends try to love
one another
at all times.

Bible Verse:
"A friend loves
at all times."
(Proverbs 17:17)

Supplies:
(for Opening a
Gift Bag)

clock or a watch

a gift bag

When they got to the zoo, Matt said he wanted to ride the train first. Even though Jackson wanted to see the seals first, Jackson said OK to the train ride. He liked making his friend happy.

Loving friend? (thumbs up)

A clown was giving out yo-yos. He only had one left. He handed it to Jackson. "We can share," Jackson told Matt.

Loving friend? (thumbs up)

When they went to look at the gorillas, the gorilla suddenly rushed up to the fence. Matt got scared and started to cry. "Baby, baby, scared of a gorilla," Jackson teased.

Loving friend? (thumbs down)

But then Jackson remembered he had cried one time in a thunderstorm. Sometimes, we just get scared, he thought. "Don't be afraid," he said to Matt. "The gorilla probably just wanted to say 'hi' to you!"

Loving friend? (thumbs up)

The bird house was really hot. Matt told Jackson that it was making him feel sick. Even though he was having fun looking at all the birds, Jackson went with Matt outside where it was cooler.

Loving friend? (thumbs up)

The pandas were rolling around as they played with one another. "They look like they're good friends, just like us! We sure have fun together!" Jackson said.

Loving friend? (thumbs up)

The boys decided to get double-decker ice cream cones. Matt's strawberry ice cream fell off his cone and plopped onto the pavement. Jackson started laughing. Then he said, "Too bad! So sad!"

Loving friend? (thumbs down)

Prayer:
God of Love, help us to be good friends who love at all times. Amen.

Jackson felt bad about being mean. He went back to the ice cream lady and explained what had happened. She gave Matt a whole new cone.

Loving friend? (thumbs up)

When it was time to leave the zoo, Jackson thanked Matt for coming with him. "You're a good friend," he said. "You made my trip to the zoo extra fun."

Loving friend? (thumbs up)

Praying About Loving Friends:

Have the children stand up.

Say: We're going to pretend we're grandfather clocks as we say the Bible verse.

Show the children how to clasp their hands together and swing their arms back and forth like the pendulum on a clock. As they swing their arms, lead them in *saying:*

Tick, tock, tick, tock,
A friend loves at all times,
Tick, tock, tick, tock.

Next ask them to bring their hands closer to their chests, folded for prayer. Pray.

Exploring:

Supplies:
(for Exploring)

copy paper
(2 sheets per child)

stapler

crayons

To make Friends at All Times Books.

Before Children's Church, make books by putting two sheets of paper together, folding them horizontally, and stapling twice along the fold. On the front of each book, print: "Friends Love" at the top and "At All Times" at the bottom.

Say: Today, you're going to make a Friends Love at All Times Book. When you are home, you can look at your book to remind you to be a good friend. You can show your book to your friends, too.

Guide the children through the steps of illustrating the book. Explain that if they cannot finish each drawing completely, they may finish the drawing at home.

Cover:

Have the children draw a heart.

First inside page (on the left): Have the children draw a sun to remind them to love their friends in the daytime. On the opposite page, have them draw a moon and stars to remind them to love their friends in the nighttime.

Ask the children to turn to the next page. Have them draw a happy face to remind them to love their friends in good times. On the next page, have them draw a sad face to remind them to love their friends in bad, sad, or mad times.

On the last two-page spread of the book, invite them to draw a scene showing friends playing together and showing love to one another. Suggestions might include: a child bringing a balloon to a sick friend; a child sharing a big cookie with a friend; a child tossing a ball to a friend; or two friends blowing bubbles together.

If time permits, encourage the children to show their completed books to one another.

Snacking With Friends:

In honor of Matt and Jackson, the two good friends in today's story, serve the children ice cream cones.

Exploring Some More:

The children will enjoy books about friendship. Consider the Arthur Books by Marc Brown, Hey, Al by Arthur Yorinks, the Frog and Toad books by Arnold Lobel, Horton Hatches the Egg by Dr. Seuss, Mike Mulligan and His Steam Shovel by Virginia Lee Burton, or one of the Winnie-the-Pooh stories by A.A. Milne. For additional titles check with the local library.

Saying Goodbye:

Ask the children to look through the pages of their Friends Love at All Times Book.

Say: It's not easy to be a loving friend every single second of the day, but God wants us to try. A friend loves at all times! Goodbye, Loving Friends!

Snack:
ice cream
ice cream cones
ice cream scoop

Supplies:
(for Exploring Some More)
picture books about friendship

Message:
Friends pray for one another.

Bible Verse:
"When I remember you in my prayers, I always thank my God."
(Philemon 1:4)

Supplies:
(for Opening a Gift Bag)

bags of pebbles

bold permanent markers

gift bag

PRAYING FRIENDS

Opening a Gift Bag:

For the Exploring activity, children will make Prayer Pebbles. Pebbles need to be large enough not to be a choking hazard. Bags of pebbles can be purchased at many craft, garden, and dollar stores. Since the children will write with markers on the pebbles, the pebbles should not be dark in color. To introduce the message, place the pebbles in a gift bag.

Gather the children together. Hold up the gift bag.

Ask: Can you guess what is in our gift bag today? Do you think it is an elephant? A volcano? A rocket?

Pull out a few of the pebbles.

Say: Pebbles! That's what is in our gift bag today! I brought pebbles because we are going to make Prayer Pebbles in a little while. One way that we can share God's love is by praying for our friends. We will make Prayer Pebbles to help us remember to pray for our friends.

Sharing a Story:

Today's story will help children understand that their friends need their prayers.

Say: In the Bible, we read about Paul. Paul and his friends traveled from place to place to tell people about Jesus and to start the Christian Church. This was hard work! They prayed for one another. Paul often wrote letters encouraging his friends. He told them he was praying for them. In one letter he wrote, "When I remember you in my prayers, I always thank my God."

God wants us to pray for our friends too. As I tell today's story, I will pause and ask you how the person in the story can help his or her friend. You will *call out the friend's name and say "I will pray for you!"*

Practice a Few Times:

Ask: How can you help Jessica? (Children will *respond: Jessica, I will pray for you.*) How can you help Lexie? (Children will *respond: Lexie, I will pray for you.*) How can you help Carlos? (Children will *respond: Carlos, I will pray for you.*)

Tell the Story:

Brady fell off the top of the slide. His arm hurt really badly. His dad rushed him to the hospital. Brady's arm was broken. How can you help Brady?

Children: *Brady, I will pray for you!*

Kallie's father lost his job. Kallie is upset because her parents seem so sad, and they are worried about paying their bills. How can you help Kallie?

Children: *Kallie, I will pray for you!*

Rodel has just moved to a new town. At school, the kids are not being very nice to him. He's having trouble making friends. How can you help Rodel?

Children: *Rodel, I will pray for you!*

Hart's big sister is being really mean. She is rude to Hart and to his parents. Everyone is upset by how she is acting. How can you help Hart?

Children: *Hart, I will pray for you!*

28

Crystal was born with a disease that makes it hard for her to walk. She needs to use a walker and has trouble keeping up with the other children at recess. Sometimes, she feels left out. How can you help Crystal?

Children: *Crystal, I will pray for you!*

Tyronne's grandma is very sick. She is too sick to come to their house anymore and too sick to play Chinese Checkers with Tyronne. How can you help Tyronne?

Children: *Tyronne, I will pray for you!*

Damaris was in a car accident. He has to wear a neck brace, and he is not allowed to go swimming. His neck hurts, and he is tired of the brace. How can you help Damaris?

Children: *Damaris, I will pray for you!*

Adair just can't learn to add. No matter how hard he tries, he keeps having trouble with math. How can you help Adair?

Children: *Adair, I will pray for you!*

Jon has a terrible temper. He gets mad and pushes other kids on the playground. Whenever he plays a game, he calls out "Cheater" if he doesn't win. At his house, he gets sent to his room for slamming doors. How can you help Jon?

Children: *Jon, I will pray for you!*

Annalisa's little brother had to go to a hospital in another city. Her mom had to go to be with him. Annalisa misses them both. How can you help Annalisa?

Children: *Annalisa, I will pray for you!*

Beth's uncle is serving overseas in the military. Beth misses him and wishes he could come home to play kickball with her again. How can you help Beth?

Children: *Beth, I will pray for you and your uncle!*

Say: When you tell people you will pray for them, it makes them feel cared for and loved. Promise all of your friends you will pray for them, especially those who need extra care and love.

Praying About Friends:

Ask the children to form a circle. Explain that during the prayer, you will go around the circle and point to each one of them. When you do, they are to say the name of one of their friends. Pray the Prayer About Friends.

Exploring:

To make Prayer Pebbles, you will need pebbles (as described in the opening) and bold permanent markers. Make a sample Prayer Pebble to show the children by drawing a smiley face on a pebble.

Show the children your Prayer Pebble.

Say: God wants us to pray for our friends. Sometimes, we get so busy that we forget to pray. Today, you are going to make a Prayer Pebble to help you remember to pray. You can keep it in your room or a place where you will see it every day. When you look at your Prayer Pebble, you will remember to pray for your friends.

Have the children draw a smiley face on their pebbles. If they choose, they may decorate the other side, too.

Invite the children to pick up their Prayer Pebbles.

Say: When you see your pebble, stop and say a prayer for a friend. You might even want to hold your pebble in your hand as you pray. And when your friends come to visit, show them your Prayer Pebble and explain that you pray for them.

Prayer About Friends:
God of Love, help us, like Paul, to pray for our friends. Today, we will pray for (point to each child). We're glad they are our friends, and we pray that they will have good days. Amen.

Supplies:
(for Exploring)

bags of pebbles (1 pebble per child)

bold permanent markers

Snack:

M & M's® or
another round or
oval-shaped candy

pudding, yogurt,
or softened ice
cream

Snacking With Friends:

In honor of the Prayer Pebbles, invite the children to stir M & M's® or another round or oval-shaped candy into pudding, yogurt, or softened ice cream.

Say: This is a fun snack to serve your friends when they come to visit!

Exploring Some More:

Lead children in the Praying Friends Cheer.

Say: We are going to cheer for our friends. We will take turns saying the name of a friend to be used each time.

(Name of friend), (raise one arm high in the air and shake)

(Name of friend), (raise the other arm high in the air and shake)

She or he is the one! (wave both arms in the air)

Let's pray for (name of friend) everyone! (hands folded in prayer above heads, sway from side to side)

God bless (name of friend)! (Clap hands high in the air.)

Invite the children to continue calling out the names of friends as long as time and energy permit.

Saying Goodbye:

Have children hold their Prayer Pebbles.

Say: You can show God's love to your friends by praying for them. Goodbye to your Prayer Pebbles, and goodbye to you!

FRIENDS BY NAME

Opening a Gift Bag:

On separate sheets of paper, use bold printing to write the names of three or four of the children. Fold the sheets of paper and put them into a gift bag.

Gather the children together. Hold up the gift bag.

Ask: Can you name what's in this bag?

Say: It's names!

Call a child one at a time to come forward, unfold a name, and hold it up. Let the other children read the name. If no one in the group can read the name, read it.

Say: Those are just a few of the names of some of our friends who come to Children's Church. Today we are going to talk about names, our names and others' names. Learning one another's names is a great way to share God's love.

Sharing a Story:

The children will hear a bit of information about names in Bible times and then answer a question each time about names today.

Tell the Story:

The Bible is filled with the names of people. Here are some of them. If you hear your name, raise your hand: Mary, Paul, Elizabeth, Noah, Matthew, Ruth, James, John, Hannah, Joshua, Jacob, Jesse, Rachel, and Lydia. These names are all in the Bible.

But there are lots of other wonderful names too. Let's each say our names.

(Let each child say his or her name.)

In Bible times, the Hebrew people usually did not have middle names. But today, most people have middle names. Let's each say our middle name.

(Let each child say her or his middle name.)

In Bible times, the Hebrew people didn't have last names. Today, people do have last names. Let's each say our last name.

(Let each child say his or her last name.)

In Bible times, instead of last names, the Hebrew people added the name of their town to their name such as Jesus of Nazareth. Let's each say the name of our town.

(Let each child say the name of his or her town or city.)

In the Bible, sometimes people's names were changed by God or by Jesus. Abram became Abraham. Sarai became Sarah. Simon became Peter. Saul became Paul. Let's each say another name that we might like to be called.

(Let each child say another name.)

Sometimes, people were called special names. Jesus gave Simon the name, "Peter," which means "rock." Does your family call you by any special names? Let's each say the name our families sometimes call us.

(Let each child say what she or he is sometimes called.)

In Bible times, people called their friends by name. In 3 John 1:15, John wrote, "Peace to you. Greet the friends there, each by name."

When you make a new friend, often the first thing you ask is, "What is your name?" Your new friend says her or his name and then asks what your name is. From then on, you know each other's names. It's important to call our friends by name. Let's each say the name of a friend.

Message:
We call one another by name.

Bible Verse:
"Peace to you. The friends send you their greetings. Greet the friends there, each by name."
(3 John 1:15)

Supplies:
(for Opening a Gift Bag)
sheets of paper
marker
a gift bag

Name Prayer:

God of Love, we're glad that we have names and that we can greet one another by name. We thank you today for everyone who is here at Children's Church. We will think about each person as we hear his or her name. (Say the name of each child.) **Hooray for names! Amen.**

Supplies:

(for Exploring)

large plastic ball

dark colored permanent marker

Snack:

1 or 2 tubes of frosting

large cookies, graham crackers, or rice cakes

Supplies:

(Exploring Some More)

notebooks

new pens or pencils

stickers

32

(Let each child say the name of a friend.)

When we greet our friends, when we pray for them, when we call them up, and when we talk about them, we use their names. Their names become special to us. One of the ways we can show our love to our friends is by calling them by name.

Praying About Names:

Ask the children to listen for each child's name as you pray the Name Prayer.

Exploring:

Children will decorate a Name Call Ball to use in a game. You will need a plastic ball. If you are not using a new ball, wash the ball ahead of time so the surface is clean.

Hold up the ball.

Say: We're going to turn this ball into a better ball by writing our names on it.

Let each child write his or her name on the ball. Assist any children who do not know how to write their names yet.

Hold up the decorated ball.

Say: Now our ball is a Name Call Ball. We'll use it to play a game called "Call Ball."

Have the children sit or stand in a circle. Explain that they are to roll the ball to someone in the circle, calling that child's name. That child is to catch the ball, then roll it to someone else, calling that child's name. Everyone should be called on once.

Snacking With Names:

Let the children watch as you write each child's name in frosting on a snack.

Exploring Some More:

Children will decorate Autograph Books, then enjoy gathering one another's signatures. Dollar stores are a good place to find inexpensive notebooks.

Children will decorate the notebook covers with stickers. If the notebooks already have decorated covers, stickers may be used to decorate some of the inside pages.

Before Children's Church, on the first page of each book, write: "This book belongs to _____." Although not necessary, a gift of a new pen or pencil will add to the fun.

Say: In the olden days, it was the style to keep an autograph book. To "autograph" something means "to write your name." People had fun signing one another's books. This way, you had a record of the names and signatures of all your friends.

Give each child a notebook. Hand out the stickers. Invite them to decorate the covers and/or the inside pages of the notebook. When the Autograph Books are finished, give each child a pen or pencil. Help them write their own names on the first page after the words "This book belongs to _____."

Invite the children to pass their books around for everyone to sign. Make sure you sign each book yourself. Explain that in the days to come, they should collect the signatures of other friends, too.

Saying Goodbye:

Have the children each touch a finger to the Name Call Ball.

Say: Greeting your friends by name is a great way to share God's love with one another! Goodbye Friends with Wonderful Names!

If the children decorated Autograph Books, remind them to take their special books home with them.

LOYAL FRIENDS

Message:
Friends are loyal.

Opening a Gift Bag:

To introduce the message, you will need a gift bag large enough to hold a toy animal. The animal will tell today's story. Place the animal in the bag.

Gather the children together. Hold up the gift bag, making it wiggle.

Say: There is something alive in this bag. Something that wants to get out! May I have a volunteer to come forward and take it out? (Choose a child to help.)

Say: Be gentle. You don't want to hurt it! I wonder what it is?

(Have the child hold up the animal.)

Ask: What it is? (*an elephant, a bear, a kitten*)

Say: It's my friend Casey! Hi Casey. Why were you in the gift bag?

(Make the animal talk in a silly voice, and move him about as you speak.)

Say: I want to tell you a story about my loyal friend Marta and me. A loyal friend is always there for you, no matter what. Do you want to hear my story?

Bible Verse:
"A true friend sticks closer than one's nearest kin." (Proverbs 18:24)

Sharing a Story:

The children will urge Casey on with his storytelling by *shouting: And then what happened Casey?* Choose a cue for the animal to give the children such as wiggling an ear, wagging a tail, or swirling through the air. Practice this, then begin.

Tell the Story: (Continue to use the animal's silly voice.)

Supplies:
(for Opening a Gift Bag and Tell the Story)

toy animal

a gift bag

One day Marta and I decided to go into the woods. We heard a loud, terrible noise. Marta let out a scream. (cue)

Children: *And then what happened Casey?*

I rushed over to Marta and gave her a hug. "Don't be scared," I said. So we kept on walking, and we ran into a gorilla. She was just calling good morning to her babies. There was nothing to worry about. Then, Marta stepped in a mess of mud and got stuck. She yelled, "I'm stuck! I'm stuck!" (cue)

Children: *And then what happened Casey?*

I took hold of Marta and pulled and pulled until we got her out of that mud! She was so happy. We went and rinsed off in the lake. Then we decided to climb a tall tree. After awhile, we came down, but Marta was afraid. She started crying. (cue)

Children: *And then what happened Casey?*

I just talked to her very calmly. I told here where to put her feet. She came down slowly, branch by branch. Just then, a giant bird came and swooped her up. "Help! Help! Casey, help me!" she called. (cue)

Children: *And then what happened Casey?*

I just called up, "Kind Bird, you have my friend Marta. I am loyal to her. I ask that you bring her back down." The bird did! So we started back on our walk, but a huge volcano began to erupt. We needed to run, but Marta was frozen with fear. (cue)

Children: *And then what happened Casey?*

I rushed back and grabbed her and we ran and ran. We ran all the way home. (cue)

Children: *And then what happened Casey?*

We had our favorite snack, cookies and milk. Marta said, "You're a good friend, Casey." I said, "I try to be. I'll stick with you forever. I'm loyal and I love you." That's why I came today. That's why I hid in the bag. So I could tell you my story!

Supplies:
(for Exploring)

fresh or artificial
ivy

copy paper

dark crayons

Snack:
sandwich cookies

napkins

Supplies:
(for Exploring
Some More)

toy animal

CD player

CD of children's
music

Praying About Loyalty:

Invite the children to line up, standing as close as they possibly can to one another.

Say: There's a verse in the Bible about friends and loyalty. This is the verse: "A true friend sticks closer than one's nearest kin" (Proverbs 18:24). Let's pray.

Exploring:

Children will make Ivy Rubbings. Cut the ivy vine apart so that each child will have a leaf. If practical, bring in a longer vine, too. If you cannot find ivy, substitute another leaf that resembles ivy.

Hold up the ivy vine (or an ivy leaf if you do not have the vine.)

Ask: Does anyone recognize this? (*Ivy*)

Say: This is ivy. Ivy is a symbol of friendship and loyalty. It grows on a vine and looks a little bit like friends in a row. Today, in honor of friendship and loyalty, you're going to make Ivy Rubbings.

Put an ivy leaf underneath a piece of paper with the veined side facing up. Show the children how to gently rub a crayon over the paper until the pattern appears.

Give each child an ivy leaf and a piece of paper. Hand out the crayons. Tell everyone to watch for the pattern of the ivy leaf as it appears. If time permits, encourage the children to move the ivy leaf to new spots under the paper, and rub with the crayon again.

Display the rubbings in your church along with a sign explaining the symbolism of ivy, or send the rubbings home with the children.

Snacking With Loyalty:

In honor of the concept of sticking together, serve the children sandwich cookies.

Say: These cookies stick together just as good friends do!

As the children enjoy their snack, ask them to share stories of their own loyalty to friends.

Exploring Some More:

The children will enjoy playing "Musical Pass the Animal" with Casey, the animal used in the story. Have the children sit or stand in a circle.

Say: Casey loves music! Let's play "Musical Pass the Animal" and let our animal friend have extra fun. We'll pass Casey around the circle. When the music stops, whoever is holding Casey will give him a big hug and *say: "I'm your friend, Casey. I'll be loyal to you!"*

Play as time permits. When the game is over, let any child who did not get a chance to hug Casey, do so now.

Saying Goodbye:

Have the children pick up their Ivy Rubbings, if you are sending the craft home.

Say: This week work extra hard to be a good, loyal friend. Remember, good friends stick together in bad times and good times, sad times and happy times. Goodbye, Loyal Friends!

JESUS AND FRIENDS

Opening a Gift Bag:

To introduce the message, place a knife, fork, spoon, and napkin in a gift bag.

Gather the children together. Hold up the gift bag.

Ask: Sometimes, it is fun to have friends come to share a meal with us at our house. Inside this bag is something you might use if you had a guest at your table. What do you think it could be? (*food, fork, napkins, plates*)

Reach into the bag and pull out each item, arranging them on a table or on the floor in front of you as you would when setting a table.

Say: Now the place is set with a knife, fork, spoon, and napkin. It is ready for a friend! And today we are going to hear a Bible story about Jesus visiting the home of a brand new friend.

Sharing a Story:

To tell the story of Jesus and Zacchaeus, use a white markerboard and marker, chalkboard and chalk, or large sheet of paper and a marker or crayon. Read over the story before Children's Church to decide how you want to space the drawings.

Tell the Story:

Say: Watch as I draw the story of Jesus and Zacchaeus.

Once upon a time there was a small man named Zacchaeus. (draw stick figure man)

He was a tax collector, which meant he collected money from people. (Draw a few dollar signs around Zacchaeus.)

That is why people did not like Zacchaeus. (Draw a few circles with frownie faces.)

One day, Zacchaeus heard that Jesus was coming to his town. He wanted to see Jesus, but there was a huge crowd. He climbed to the top of a tree. (Draw a simple tree, and put a stick figure of Zacchaeus in the top.)

When Jesus came by... (Draw a stick figure at the bottom of the tree.)

He looked up and said, "Zacchaeus, you come down. I am going to your house today."

So Zacchaeus climbed down from the tree, and Jesus went to the house of his brand new friend. (Draw a table with Zacchaeus on one side and Jesus on the other. Put a few bowls on the table.)

Even though Zacchaeus was a tax collector and took money from people, Jesus cared about him. Jesus was his friend. Jesus made friends with lots of people, and Zacchaeus was one of them. (Draw a large heart around Jesus and Zacchaeus.)

The End.

Next, teach children the song, "Zacchaeus." If you are not familiar with the tune, you can invite them to say, instead of sing, the words, as you lead them in the actions.

Sing:

Zacchaeus was a wee little man, (left palm up with right palm above it, as if measuring)

A wee little man was he. (palms closer)

He climbed up in a sycamore tree, (alternate hands as if climbing)

For the Lord he wanted to see. (hand to shade eyes, look down)

And as the Savior passed that way, (swing arms as if walking)

Message:
Jesus made friends.

Bible Verse:
"When Jesus came to the place, he looked up and said to him, 'Zacchaeus, hurry and come down; for I must stay at your house today.'" (Luke 19:5)

Supplies:
(for Opening a Gift Bag)

knife

fork

spoon

napkin

a gift bag

Supplies:
(for Sharing a Story and Tell the Story)

white markerboard and marker

or

chalkboard and chalk

or

large sheet of paper and marker or crayon

He looked up in the tree, (hand to shade eyes, look up)
(Spoken) **And he said, "Zacchaeus, you come down,** (beckon with hand)
For I'm going to your house today, (clap in rhythm)
For I'm going to your house today." (clap in rhythm)
(Words based on Luke 19:1-5. Music: Traditional.)

Praying About Jesus and Zacchaeus:

Have children repeat each line of the prayer after you. Pray.

Prayer:
God of Love,
Thanks for Jesus,
(children repeat)
Who made friends
with Zacchaeus.
(children repeat)
And thanks for
Zacchaeus,
(children repeat)
Who made friends
with Jesus.
(children repeat)
Amen.
(children repeat)

Exploring:

Children will make Friendly Placemats to use when a new friend comes to their house.

Plain placemats can often be purchased in packs of twenty or more in party stores and paper good departments. If you cannot locate these, shelf paper or wallpaper can be cut into rectangles about the size of a standard placemat. You can also use a sheet of construction paper. Children will decorate their placemats with one large doily or several smaller doilies.

Say: Zacchaeus welcomed Jesus into his home. It's fun to welcome new friends to our homes! Today, you are going to decorate a placemat to use the next time a new friend visits your house.

Give each child a placemat and one or several doilies. Explain that they are to glue the doily/doilies on top of the placemat. If the placemats are white, you might want to have the children color them with bright colors first. Once the doilies are in place, invite the children to decorate the placemats any way they like.

Say: The next time a new friend comes to your house, welcome your friend just as Zacchaeus welcomed Jesus. Enjoy serving a snack or meal to your new friend on top of your beautiful placemat.

Supplies:
(for Exploring)
placemats
paper doilies
glue
crayons

Snacking With Jesus:

Before you serve the snack, let the children watch as you set an extra place.

Say: In some families, it's a tradition to set a place for Jesus. Even though Jesus doesn't really come and sit at the table, it's a way to remember that he is our friend. We know that he loves us and cares for us just as he did for his Bible friends.

As children enjoy their snack, ask them to tell about a time when someone came to their house to share a meal.

Snack:
crackers
cheese slices
seedless grapes
(cut in half)
raisins
extra place setting

Exploring Some More:

Children will enjoy using play clay to make a Pretend Meal for a friend.

Purchase the clay or make your own (see page 19). Provide several colors.

Give each child a paper plate, and set out the play clay. Invite the children to create a delicious Pretend Meal to serve to a friend.

When the children have finished, let them take turns showing the foods they prepared. Send the Pretend Meals home with children, if practical.

Saying Goodbye:

Have the children hold their placemats.

Say: Remember to make new friends and to be good to your old friends, too. What a happy way to share God's love! Goodbye, Good Friends!

If you made Pretend Meals and have decided to send them home, have the children take those, too.

Supplies:
(for Exploring
Some More)
play clay
paper plates

36

Younger Friends, Older Friends

Opening a Gift Bag:

To introduce the message, place birthday candles in a gift bag. Gather the children together. Hold up the gift bag.

Say: I'm going to give you a hint as to what is in this bag. Are you one? Are you two? Are you three? Are you four? Are you five? Are you six? Are you seven?

Ask: Can anyone guess what's in the bag? (*birthday candles, birthday stuff, birthday presents*)

Pull out the candles.

Ask: What are these? (*birthday candles*) What do we do with them? (*We put them on birthday cakes and light them.*)

Say: Usually there is one candle on a cake for each year of a person's life. Sometimes, there is an extra one to grow on. When you are little, you have just a few candles on your cake. When you get older, there are more candles. When you are really, really old, there are lots of candles on your cake.

Ask: Do any of you have friends who are really little? Babies or toddlers? Do any of you have friends who are really, really old? As old as your grandmas and grandpas and even older?

Say: We can share God's love with friends who are young and friends who are old!

Sharing a Story:

Children will participate in the story by singing "Happy Birthday" on cue, adding the person's name used in that part of the story. Practice this a few times and then begin.

Tell the Story:

The Children's Church kids are friends with one another. They have a good time because they are all about the same age and like to do many of the same things. At church, the kids also have some friends who are really young and some friends who are very old. Let us help the kids out by singing along with them at some of their church activities.

One Sunday, the kids find out that Jeremy, a baby boy in their church, has just turned one. "Happy Birthday, Jeremy," one of the boys says. "We will sing for you." Let us help the kids sing "Happy Birthday" to Jeremy. (*all sing*)

Then, they find out that Trev's second birthday is on Wednesday. "Let us sing to Trev," a girl says. Let us help the kids sing "Happy Birthday" to Trev. (*all sing*)

Mrs. Wellington is very old. She has to walk with the help of a walker. She hears the Children's Church kids singing and says, "My birthday is next week, too. I'll be ninety-one." "Happy birthday!" one of the girls says. "We will sing to you!" Let us help the kids sing "Happy Birthday" to Mrs. Wellington. (*all sing*)

"Birthdays," said Mr. Sanchez, who looks even older than Mrs. Wellington. "I cannot even remember when mine is!" "Well, then we will sing to you right now!" one of the boys tells him. Let us help the kids sing to Mr. Sanchez. (*all sing*)

A little girl, about eighteen months old is standing in the hallway. "Birffday, birffday. Sing to me, sing to me." Her dad smiles and says, "Julie, your birthday is not for six

Message:
We share God's love with the young and the old.

Bible Verse:
"I have been young, and now am old." (Psalm 37:25)

Supplies:
(for Opening a Gift Bag)

birthday candles

a gift bag

Prayer:

God of Love, please help us share your love with kids who are babies and toddlers like the one we are picturing in our minds right now.
(pause)
And please help us to share your love with grownups who are older like the person we are picturing in our minds right now.
(pause)
We know that little children and older people especially need our love.
Amen.

Supplies:

(for Exploring)

posterboard in a bright color

copy paper

scissors

a dark marker

crayons

glue or tape

---

whole months." "We will sing for her anyway," one of the girls says. "Sure," says a boy. Let's help the kids sing to Julie. (*all sing*)

Mr. Jonas is blind. His daughter brings him to church. He lost his eyesight from an eye disease when he was in his eighties. He cannot see the kids, but he can hear their singing. "Beautiful," he tells them. "We will sing for you, Mr. Jonas," one of the boys says. "No matter when your birthday is!" Let us help the kids sing to Mr. Jonas. (*all sing*)

A mom and dad come in carrying their brand new baby. No one at church has seen him before. All the kids rush over to have a look. "He was just born a week ago," the dad announces proudly. "Then he deserves a birthday song for being born!" says one of the girls. "His name is Griffin," says the mom. Let us help the kids sing to Griffin. (*all sing*)

And that is the story of the Children's Church kids and their friends, young and old. Singing "Happy Birthday" is just one of the ways the kids share their love with the babies and toddlers and the elderly at their church.

Praying About Younger and Older Friends:

Explain to the children that during the prayer, you will first ask them to picture the face of someone they know who is young and then the face of someone they know who is old now. Ask them to close their eyes. Pray.

Exploring:

Children will make a Bow Wow Poster to decorate the church nursery. A large group might want to have the children create more than one poster.

Before Children's Church, write: "Bow Wow!" at the top of the posterboard and "Love, The Children's Church Kids" at the bottom.

The poster will feature dog faces the children create with paper and crayons. Prepare the paper ahead of time. To create a square, fold the paper down from one of the top corners to the opposite side. Trim off the remaining strip. Fold each square in half to form a triangle. Cut at least one square for each child and visitor.

Before class, make a sample dog face to show the class. On the long side of the triangle, fold the paper down to form long ears (Step 5). Fold the top and bottom points back to create the dog's chin and the top of the dog's head (Step 6). Use crayons to add the eyes, nose, mouth, whiskers, and any other details such as spots or curly hair.

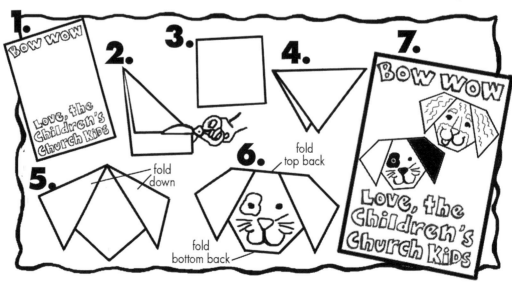

Ask: When children are little, we teach them animal sounds. When we ask them who says, "Bow wow!" What do they answer? (*a dog*)

Hold up the sample dog face.

Say: We are going to make these paper dog faces to create a Bow Wow Poster to decorate the church nursery.

As children complete their dog faces, glue or tape the faces to the poster. If practical, let the children help deliver the Bow Wow Poster to the nursery. If not, deliver the poster at another time.

Snacking With Birthday Cake:

In honor of our love for young and old, enjoy a decorated birthday cake or decorated cupcakes. Lead the children in singing "Happy Birthday" one more time, using "Everyone" when it's time to fill in the name.

As children enjoy the snack, ask them to tell how old they will be on their next birthday.

Exploring Some More:

To make Bow Wow Birthday Cards. See supplies list.

Before Children's Church, prepare the paper as explained in Exploring (see page 38).

Say: We're going to make Bow Wow Birthday cards to send to an elderly member of our congregation.

Have the children fold construction paper in half to form a card. Then have them create a paper dog face and attach the dog face to the card. Write, or have the children write, "Bow Wow! Happy Birthday" on the inside of their cards. Ask them to sign their names. Explain that you will mail the Bow Wow Birthday cards to an elderly member of your congregation on his or her birthday.

Saying Goodbye:

Ask the children to use their fingers to show how old they are.

Say: Remember that your age is a perfect age for showing love to those who are younger and those who are much older than you are! Goodbye, (Name the ages of the children) Year-olds!

Snack:
birthday cake or
cupcakes

Supplies:
(for Exploring
Some More)
construction paper
copy paper
scissors or
paper cutter
crayons
glue, tape,
or stapler

39

Bible Verse:
"The gifts he
gave were that
some would
be apostles,
some prophets,
some evangelists,
some pastors
and teachers."
(Ephesians 4:11)

Supplies:
(for Opening
a Gift Bag)

borrow an item
from your pastor
such as a liturgical
stole, a cross,
a trinket from his
or her desk or
something else
that represents
the role of the
pastor

photo of
your pastor

(Many church
directories have
photos of
the pastor.)

a gift bag

THE PASTOR

Opening a Gift Bag:

To introduce the message, borrow an item from your pastor to tuck into the gift bag. Gather the children together. Hold up the gift bag.

Say: I have something in this bag that represents someone who is our friend.

Ask: Can you guess who this belongs to? (*Pastor Shultz; our minister, Dr. Bob*)

Explain the significance of the item. Next, if you located a photo of your pastor, show it to the children.

Ask: Why is the pastor our friend? (*He prays for us. She teaches us about God.*)

Say: A pastor leads and cares for the members of a church. A pastor teaches, preaches, guides, and comforts. Our pastor helps us remember that God is with us at all times to love us and care for us. Our pastor is our friend.

Sharing a Story:

Ask the children the following Pastor Riddles. Lead them in acting out the answer.

Tell the Story:

Say: I am going to ask you some Pastor Riddles. Each one asks a question about something pastors do. Once you solve the riddle, we'll act out the answer together.

Riddle: This is something pastors do when visiting sick people, leading a worship service, before a church supper, or when they are alone. What is it?

Answer: *Pray.*

(Have the children fold their hands in prayer.)

Riddle: This is something pastors do when they are studying to be a pastor, when they are preparing a sermon, and during the worship service. Of course, they do this lots of other times, too.

Answer: *Read from the Bible.*

(Have the children pretend to hold a Bible and **repeat with you: In the beginning God created the heaven and the earth.**)

Riddle: This is something pastors do when people join the church, when people are sick, or when people are sad. Usually, they need their cars to do this. What is it?

Answer: *Visit people.*

(Have the children pretend to drive a car. Then have them pretend to honk their horns as they **call out: Beep, beep!**)

Riddle: This is something pastors do when they are standing in the pulpit delivering a sermon. Their words help us understand more about God. What is it?

Answer: *Preach.*

(Have the children pretend to stand in a pulpit. They can use their arms to gesture.)

Riddle: This is something pastors do when the worship service is over, when they meet new people, and when we see them in the hall. What is it?

Answer: *Shake hands or give hugs, and say, "Hello! Good to see you!"*

(Have the children pretend to shake hands. Next, have them give pretend hugs. Lead them in **calling out: Hello! Good to see you!**)

You did a good job answering the Pastor Riddles and acting out some of the things that pastors do.

Praying for Our Pastor:

Say: There's a verse in the Bible that talks about the gifts God gives to people. God gives some the ability to be a good pastor. (Read today's Bible verse.)

Ask: What is our pastor's name? Can you tell me some things about our pastor? *(She has red hair. He sings well. He can throw a football far.)*

Ask: What are some of the ways we can share God's love with our pastor? *(prayers, cards, cookies, kind words, enthusiasm, support)*

Say: Let us say the Pastor Prayer. Pray with the children.

Exploring:

Children will make a Thumbody Poster for your pastor. If you have more than one pastor, make a poster for each one, or let them share the poster.

Before Children's Church, at the top of the poster write: "(Pastor's title and name), Thumbodies Who Love You!" Use a pencil to draw a large heart in the center. Leave room at the bottom for the children to make additional thumbprints and sign their first names.

Say: Our pastor is our friend. Today, we are going to make him or her a Thumbody Poster as a surprise.

Show how to press your thumb onto the inkpad, and then onto the outline of the heart.

Say: That's a thumbody!

Invite the children to take turns adding a thumbody to the outline of the heart. Continue until the heart is outlined with thumbprints. If time permits, the children can make thumbprints to fill in the heart, too.

Next, have them each make their thumbprint on the bottom section of the poster. Have them sign their names next to their thumbprint. Help those who cannot write yet.

If practical, have the children help deliver the poster to the pastor.

Snacking With the Pastor's Snack:

Check with your pastor to learn one of his or her favorite snacks.

Say: Guess what! In honor of our pastor, today we are going to enjoy one of his or her favorite snacks! He or she loves it because (fill in the pastor's response).

Exploring Some More:

Sing this song to the tune of "This Is the Way We Wash Our Clothes":

Sing: *This is the way our pastor preaches, pastor preaches, pastor preaches. This is the way our pastor preaches.* (make gestures of a pastor preaching) *Our pastor is our friend.* (arms outstretched)

This is the way our pastor prays, pastor prays, pastor prays. This is the way our pastor prays. (hands folded in prayer) *Our pastor is our friend.* (arms outstretched)

This is the way our pastor sings, pastor sings, pastor sings. This is the way our pastor sings. (Sing: *La, la, la*) *Our pastor is our friend.* (arms outstretched)

Invite the children to think more verses and actions.

Saying Goodbye:

Say: It was fun making a Thumbody Poster for our pastor. Being kind and friendly to our pastor is a good way to share God's love. Goodbye, Thumbodies!

Sharing God's Love With Friends

God of Love, thank you for our pastor (name). Be with her or him as she or he teaches, preaches, guides, and comforts. We are glad our pastor is our friend. Amen.

Supplies:

(for Exploring)

posterboard in a light color

pencil

inkpad

markers

paper towels, or moist towelettes

Snack:

the pastor's favorite snacks

Chapter 3

Sharing God's Love AT CHURCH

Message:
Christians come together at church.

Bible Verse:
"All who believed were together."
(Acts 2:44)

Supplies:
(for Opening the Bible)
NRSV Bible
construction paper
scissors
pencil
crayons

BELIEVERS TOGETHER

Opening the Bible:

To introduce the message, tuck the paper doll people into a Bible. To make paper doll people, fold a piece of paper into a fan the size you want the dolls to be. Draw a simple doll shape with two arms and legs extending out from the body onto the folds. Cut around the doll shape, being careful not to snip the folds at the arms and legs. Unfold. Decorate if you wish. Place the paper doll people in a Bible.

be careful not to snip the fold at the arms and legs

Gather the children together. Hold up the Bible for all to see.

Say: This is the Bible: the Word of God for the people of God.

Open the Bible and pull out the paper doll people.

Ask: What's this? (*people holding hands, paper dolls, a chain of people*)

Say: These people are Christians. Christians are joined together because they believe in Jesus Christ. Christians are known as People of the Word. This means their faith comes from the Bible.

Ask: Where do Christian people come together to study the Bible and to worship God? (*Church*)

Say: Yes, people who believe in Jesus Christ want to be together at church. In churches, Christians sing and pray, listen and learn, work on projects, laugh and talk, support one another in times of happiness and sadness; and help people in their communities and around the world. As Christians, we share God's love by coming together at church.

Sharing a Story:

The focus of this story is the beginning of the early church (Acts 2). The children will punctuate the end of each line by stomping their feet twice and then clapping twice. Lead them by stomping and clapping along with them. Practice this a few times and begin.

Tell the Story:

The Holy Spirit came (stomp, stomp; clap, clap)
And touched the apostles. (stomp, stomp; clap, clap)

A crowd heard Peter preach (stomp, stomp; clap, clap)
Then they became believers. (stomp, stomp; clap, clap)

They believed in Jesus (stomp, stomp; clap, clap)
And were baptized in the water. (stomp, stomp; clap, clap)

Three thousand joined the church (stomp, stomp; clap, clap)
And learned Jesus' teachings. (stomp, stomp; clap, clap)

Believers were amazed (stomp, stomp; clap, clap)
As apostles worked wonders. (stomp, stomp; clap, clap)

These Christians cared and shared (stomp, stomp; clap, clap)
Giving help to the needy. (stomp, stomp; clap, clap)

Day by day by day (stomp, stomp; clap, clap)
They spent time together (stomp, stomp; clap, clap)

Going to the Temple (stomp, stomp; clap, clap)|
To pray and praise the Lord. (stomp, stomp; clap, clap)

In homes breaking bread, (stomp, stomp; clap, clap)
They ate like one big family. (stomp, stomp; clap, clap)

Glad and generous hearts (stomp, stomp; clap, clap)
Showed their good will.(stomp, stomp; clap, clap)

The Lord brought them together (stomp, stomp; clap, clap)
Linked by faith in Jesus. (stomp, stomp; clap, clap)

This is the story (stomp, stomp; clap, clap)
Of the first Christians. (stomp, stomp; clap, clap)

Praying About Believers:

Hold up the paper doll people again. Challenge the children to stand, like the paper people, touching one another, foot to foot and hand to hand. Pray the Christian Prayer.

Exploring:

Children will have fun making Believers Together Cut-outs. Choose the option that fits your time and number of children. You may want to recruit a helper or two.

Child Cut-outs:

Trace each child's head and outstretched arms onto a roll of craft paper. After you trace each child, cut the section from the roll. Invite the children to color the tracing with crayons.

Next have the children cut out the tracing and print their name. (Young children might need assistance.) When all of the cut-outs are ready, join them with tape, hand to hand. Display the large garland with a sign saying: Believers Together!

Christian Prayer:

God of Love, we stand together as believers in Jesus Christ. Thank you for Jesus and for the early church. Amen.

Supplies:

(for Exploring, Child Cut-outs)

a roll of craft paper

crayons

a large pair of scissors

masking tape

43

Supplies:
(for Exploring,
Paper Doll People)

craft or parcel
paper
(or grocery bags)

scissors

markers or
crayons

masking tape

Snack:
paper plates

marker

gingerbread man
cookies
or
gingerbread man
cookie cutter

slices of
sandwich bread

butter

cinnamon sugar

Paper Doll People:

Craft or parcel paper is sturdy, as are grocery bags with the bottoms cut away.

Before Children's Church, following the steps given in the opening activity, fold sheets of paper into fans, one per child. Trace the paper doll figures onto the fans. If you have children with good scissor skills, have them cut out the paper dolls themselves, being careful not to snip the fold points. Otherwise, cut out the paper dolls before Children's Church and refold them.

Have the children decorate their paper doll people using markers or crayons. Join the chains into one long garland for display, or allow the children to take them home.

Say: The Bible says that all believers came together in the early Christian Church.

Ask: Why do Christians come together at church? (*sing, pray, visit, help, worship*)

Say: We are joined together by our belief in Jesus. The church is the place where we meet with other believers.

Snacking With Believers:

Here are several ways to carry today's theme into the snack.

1) Buy gingerbread man cookies, if available; or bake your own.
2) Use a gingerbread man cookie cutter to cut shapes out of slices of sandwich bread. Top the cut-outs with butter and cinnamon sugar, and then toast. (The remaining bread can be toasted into croutons.)
3) Trace a paper doll person onto specially decorated paper plates.

Exploring Some More:

Teach children the familiar finger rhyme, "Here Is the Church."

Here is the church, (hands folded with fingers tucked in)

Here is the steeple, (pointer fingers form steeple)

Open the doors, (thumbs apart)

And see all the people! (open hands wide and wiggle fingers)

Next, teach them this ending:

Close the doors, (thumbs together)

And hear them pray, (place hands, still folded, to ears)

Open the doors, (thumbs apart)

And they all walk away. (take hands apart, make the fingers walk away)

Say: Christians around the world come together in all kinds of churches. There are churches with domes and spires, old churches with painted ceilings or tombs inside, simple churches with shingled steeples, round churches, cross-shaped churches, churches with stained-glass windows or statues, churches in shopping malls, and churches made from every kind of building material.

Lead the children in a discussion about the appearance of your church, inside and out.

Say: Inside Christian churches there are people young and old, rich and poor, and every color. We are believers together!

Lead the children in naming some of the members in your church and their qualities.

Saying Goodbye:

If you are sending home the Paper Doll People, have the children hold them.

Say: As Christians, we share God's love by coming together at church. Thank you for coming today. We miss you when you are not with us. Goodbye, Believers!

SING PRAISES

Opening the Bible:

To introduce the message, tuck a paper music note into a Bible. To prepare, draw a large music note on a sheet of paper. Cut the note out and place it in the first page of Psalms.

Gather the children together. Hold up the Bible for all to see.

Say: The Bible holds the words to many songs.

Open the Bible to Psalms. Take out the music note.

Ask: What's this? (*a music note*)

Say: When we see a music note, we know it is a sign for music. That's why we found the music note next to the book of Psalms. (Show the children the heading for Psalms.) "Psalm" is an Old Testament word for "song." The Book of Psalms has 150 songs in it. In Bible times, people sang the psalms to God.

Turn some of the pages for the children, showing them the psalms.

Ask: Do we sing praises to God? (*Yes, when we sing hymns and songs.*) **Where do we sing hymns and songs?** (*in Children's Church, in the worship service, in Bible School, at home*) **What do these hymns and songs say?** (*Thanks and praise to God. We love God, and God loves us. They talk about Jesus and our Christian faith.*)

Say: Since Bible times, people have been praising God with songs. We praise God with songs, too.

Sharing a Story:

For today's story, the children will hear passages from three Psalms. As you read, children will listen for four key words. When they hear these words, they are to raise their hands above their heads. You may want to ask an older child to lead the group by having the child raise the music note in one hand.

Tell the Story:

I am going to read to you three Psalms that talk about praising God with singing and musical instruments. Raise your hands high in the air when you hear the words "sing," "singing," "Lord," and "God." (Have the children repeat the words after you to help them recognize the words before you begin.) **Ready?**

Psalm 92:1-4: It is good to give thanks to the LORD, to SING praises to your name, O Most High; to declare your steadfast love in the morning, and your faithfulness by night, to the music of the lute and the harp, to the melody of the lyre. For you, O LORD, have made me glad by your work; at the works of your hands I SING for joy.

Psalm 96:1-4: O SING to the LORD a new song; SING to the LORD, all the earth. SING to the LORD, bless his name; tell of his salvation from day to day. Declare his glory among the nations, his marvelous works among all the peoples. For great is the LORD, and greatly to be praised.

Psalm 100: Make a joyful noise to the LORD, all the earth. Worship the LORD with gladness; come into his presence with SINGING. Know that the LORD is GOD. It is he that made us, and we are his; we are his people, and the sheep of his pasture. Enter his gates with thanksgiving, and his courts with praise. Give thanks to him, bless his name. For the LORD is good; his steadfast love endures forever, and his faithfulness to all generations.

What wonderful songs those are that sing praises to God!

Message:
We sing praises to God.

Bible Verse:
"It is good to give thanks to the LORD, to sing praises to your name, O Most High." (Psalm 92:1)

Supplies:
(for Opening the Bible)
NRSV Bible
sheet of paper
scissors
marker

Supplies:

(for Exploring)

white fluted
paper plates

crepe paper
streamers in one
or more colors

scissors

crayons

stapler or tape

yardstick

CD of
children's
Christian music

Snack:

O-shaped cereal

Supplies:

(for Exploring
Some More)

musician or
choir member

If time permits, read the story again as children raise their arms in the air at the appropriate words.

Praying About Praising:

Show the children how to raise their arms above their heads and sway them from side to side. Have them do this as you lead them in singing the Doxology, "Praise God, from Whom All Blessings Flow." Sing the Doxology.

Exploring:

Children will make Praise Plates to wave as they sing praises to God.

Before Children's Church, cut crepe paper streamers into 24-inch lengths. You will need six streamers for each child. Make a sample Praise Plate to show the children. Color a bright design on both sides of a paper plate. Staple or tape six 24-inch streamers around the edges of the plate.

To begin, hold up the Praise Plate.

Say: Singers and dancers sometimes wave streamers when they dance. The streamers are fun to wave, and they make the singing and dancing very festive. Today, you are going to make a Praise Plate to wave as you sing and dance.

Give each child a paper plate. Invite the children to color bright, happy designs. Next, assist them in stapling or taping six streamers around the edge of their plates.

Play the Christian music. Invite the children to sing along and dance as they wave their Praise Plates. Join in the festivities and sing and dance, too.

If the children are familiar with the CD, let them choose some of their favorite songs.

Say: It is good to sing our praises to God!

Snacking With "O" Shapes:

Serve O-shaped cereal in celebration of singing. First ask the children to watch your lips as you sing "blessings flow," "here below," and "heavenly host."

Ask: Did you see my lips make an O shape?

Demonstrate again if children have trouble with the idea.

Say: In paintings and on statues, singers are often shown with O-shaped mouths. Now you know why! To celebrate singing praises to God, I brought you some delicious, O-shaped cereal.

Exploring Some More:

Introduce the children to a musician or choir member in the congregation.

Invite your guest to play or sing a song or two, and to answer some questions like: How long have you been playing this instrument/singing? What do you enjoy most about playing/singing? Do you have a favorite hymn, praise song, or other piece of religious music? How does playing/singing make you feel inside? Do you have a funny story about playing/singing?

Encourage the children to ask their own questions. Thank your guest for sharing his or her time and talent!

Saying Goodbye:

Have the children pick up their Praise Plates.

Say: We celebrate God's love when we sing praises. Let's all *shout together: We praise God!* (all repeat) **Goodbye, Singers!**

FAMILY OF FAITH

Opening the Bible:

To introduce the message, place a paper hand in the Bible. Prepare by tracing your own hand onto a sheet of paper, cutting it out, and placing it in a Bible.

Gather the children together. Hold up the Bible for all to see.

Say: This is a Bible. It tells us what Christians should do. In Galatians it says, "Let us work for the good of all, and especially for those of the family of faith" (Galatians 6:10).

Ask: What is the name of our church?

Say: We are a family of faith. We share our faith in Jesus Christ. People who go to church together are like family. They love and care for one another like a family.

Take the paper hand out of the Bible.

Ask: What's this? *(a hand)* What are some good things hands can do? *(wave hello, color a pretty picture, fold in prayer)*

Say: People in our church family use their hands to help others in our church. There are many ways we can help one another as we share God's love.

Sharing a Story:

Use objects to help tell the story of how we can help people in our church family. Before Children's Church, collect the listed objects and place them in a shopping bag.

Tell the Story:

In this shopping bag are some objects people can use to help others. Our story today tells how the objects helped a family of faith, a church.

Pull out the car keys from the bag.

Ask: What are these? *(keys)* What are they used for? *(to start a car)*

Say: These are Mrs. Brown's car keys. She helps by driving a woman who is blind to church and by delivering food to the food bank. She drives the youth on trips. Mrs. Brown's keys help the family of faith.

Pull out a cell phone.

Ask: What's this? *(cell phone)* What is it used for? *(to call people)*

Say: This is Mr. Crane's phone. He travels with his job and uses his phone to talk to people in his church family. He calls to plan projects, to check on sick friends, and to tell jokes to cheer up another friend. Mr. Crane's phone helps the family of faith.

Pull out the hammer.

Ask: What's this? *(a hammer)* What is it used for? *(to drive nails, to fix things)*

Say: Dr. Nesbit likes to help at church by fixing things. He has fixed a railing and turned an old shed into a workroom. Dr. Nesbit's hammer helps the family of faith.

Pull out the dollar bill.

Ask: What's this? *(money, a dollar)* What is it used for? *(to buy things)*

Say: Mr. Cliff gives money to a special fund at church every week. When people in the church or the community need help because something has happened, and they can't pay their bills; the money from the fund helps the family of faith.

Pull out the greeting card.

Ask: What's this? *(a card)* What is it used for? *(to send to someone)*

Say: Mrs. Morgan loves to send greeting cards to people in the church. She sends

Message:

We help people in our church family.

Bible Verse:

"Let us work for the good of all, and especially for those of the family of faith." (Galatians 6:10)

Supplies:

(for Opening the Bible)

paper

scissors

marker

NRSV Bible

Supplies:

(for Sharing a Story)

car keys

cell phone

hammer

dollar bill

greeting card

casserole dish or disposable food storage container

work gloves

shopping bag

get-well cards to cheer up the sick, sympathy cards to comfort the sad, and birthday cards to send a smile to young and old. Mrs. Morgan's cards help the family of faith.

Pull out the dish or container.

Ask: What's this? (*dish/container*) What is it used for? (*to hold food*)

Say: Mrs. Latta makes meals for people in the church. If there is a death, illness, or new baby in the church family, Mrs. Latta brings a delicious dinner to those in need. She delivers the dinner in dishes. Mrs. Latta's dishes help the family of faith.

Pull out the work gloves.

Ask: What are these? (*work gloves*) What are they used for? (*to work outdoors*)

Say: If there is a windstorm or an ice storm, Mr. Taitt helps clean up the mess at church. Mr. Taitt likes a safe outdoors. Mr. Taitt's gloves help the family of faith.

Hold up the shopping bag.

Ask: What's this? (*shopping bag*) What is it used for? (*It holds things you buy.*)

Say: Ms. Ely has lots of shopping bags. She brings a bag full of craft supplies for the women's group. She brings bags of groceries for the spaghetti dinner. She brings a bag of Bibles for the third graders. Ms. Ely's shopping bags help the family of faith.

Keys, phones, hammers, money, cards, dishes, gloves, and shopping bags help church families everywhere, especially here at (name of your church.)

Praying About Helping:

Have the children hold out their hands, palms up to pray the Family of Faith Prayer.

Exploring:

Spread a little cheer with Thinking of You Greeting Cards. The cards can be directed to one person or several. Consider those in your congregation who are sick or lonely.

Explain to the children who you will be sending the cards to and why. Then invite everyone to create pretty or funny Thinking of You Greeting Cards. Ask children who can write to print the words, "Thinking of You" on their cards. Sign the cards.

Admire each greeting card, and invite the child who created it to comment on their design. Send the cards off, along with a note explaining that the cards come with plenty of love from the Children's Church Kids.

Snacking With Helpers:

Invite some active members of your congregation to come to Children's Church.

As everyone snacks, ask the guests to explain how they help your family of faith.

Exploring Some More:

Does your church have a photo album of events? Does your church directory have photos of church projects and activities? Could your snack time guests bring along some photos of the work they do at church?

Use the photos to show the children the church family in action. Identify people, tell stories, and point out the many ways that people are helping in the photos.

Saying Goodbye:

Invite the children to hold hands or to give one another high fives.

Say: Thank you for using your hands today to make wonderful Thinking of You Greeting Cards. Letting others know you care about them is a great way to share God's love in church. Goodbye, Helpers!

Family of Faith Prayer:
God of Love, may our hands be helping hands, working for the good of all, and especially for our family of faith. Amen.

Supplies:
(for Exploring)
light colored paper
markers or crayons
stickers (optional)

Snack:
biscuits and cream cheese or jelly

Supplies:
(for Exploring Some More)
photos of your church family in action

48

PRAY LIKE THIS

Opening the Bible:

To introduce today's message, tuck a paper pretzel into a Bible. Draw a traditional two-looped, heart-shaped pretzel onto a sheet of paper. Place the drawing in a Bible.

Gather the children together. Hold up the Bible for all to see.

Say: There are many prayers in the Bible. Since Bible days, children and grownups have been praying to God. Some of these prayers were learned and remembered.

Pull out the paper pretzel.

Ask: What's this? (*a pretzel*)

Say: An old story says that pretzels were created as little rewards for children who learned their prayers. During the Middle Ages, many people folded their arms across their chests with their hands on their shoulders when they prayed. (demonstrate) The pretzel shape looks like arms folded this way. (Hold up the pretzel with the two loops down.) This reward and treat was so popular that we still enjoy it today.

Sharing a Story:

In a story from Matthew 6:5-13, Jesus teaches his disciples to pray. The children will participate by *saying: Teach us to pray,* taken from Luke 11:1. Use the paper pretzel to cue the children. Practice this a few times and then begin.

Tell the Story:

Jesus taught his disciples a lot. Jesus taught while he walking on a road or sitting in the Temple. One day the disciples wanted to know if Jesus would…(Hold up pretzel.)

All: *Teach us to pray.*

Jesus began teaching about prayer. He told his disciples that they did not need to use a lot of big, impressive words to pray. He told them that God understand them without using big words. Jesus also said not to pray to impress people. (Hold up pretzel.)

All: *Teach us to pray.*

Jesus told the disciples to go into a room, close the door, and pray in private because God knows what is done in private and would reward them. (Hold up pretzel.)

All: *Teach us to pray.*

Jesus taught the disciples the Lord's Prayer. It goes like this:

> Our Father, who art in heaven, hallowed be thy name.
> Thy kingdom come.
> Thy will be done, on earth as it is in heaven.
> Give us this day our daily bread.
> And forgive us our trespasses, as we forgive those who trespass against us.
> And lead us not into temptation, but deliver us from evil.
> For thine is the kingdom, and the power, and the glory forever. Amen.

From the United Methodist Hymnal (895)

Let's practice saying Jesus' prayer! I'll say a line and then we will repeat it together.

(Lead the children in saying the prayer.)

Long ago, this prayer was written down so many people could learn it. The Lord's Prayer is a prayer you can learn and remember too.

Message:
Jesus teaches us to pray.

Bible Verse:
"Lord, teach us to pray." (Luke 11:1)

Supplies:
(for Opening the Bible)

paper

marker

NRSV Bible

Recipe:
(for Play Clay)

1 cup flour

1/2 cup salt

2 tsp. cream of tartar

food coloring

1 Tbsp. of vegetable oil

1 cup water

Mix the dry ingredients. Add food coloring. Add oil and water. Cook over medium heat for several minutes.

Let cool and knead. Stores well in air-tight container.

The Lord's Prayer:

say The Lord's Prayer.
Close by saying:
And let all the children say, *"Amen."*

Supplies:

(for Exploring)

a copy
of the Lord's
Prayer on colored
copy paper
(1 per child)

construction paper

glue

stickers (religious-
themed stickers,
foil star stickers,
or round
label stickers)

Snack:

traditional shape
pretzels or large
soft pretzels

Supplies:

(for Exploring
Some More)

play clay

traditional-shaped
pretzels

paper plates

50

Praying Like Jesus:

Have the children make praying arms, pretzel-style, as you again lead them in saying The Lord's Prayer. Close by **saying: And let all the children say, "Amen."**

Exploring:

The children will make small Lord's Prayer Posters to take home.

Before Children's Church, type The Lord's Prayer in a large font. Print out a copy on copy paper for each child. Stickers can be found where office supplies are sold.

Give each child a copy of the prayer, and set out the glue. Direct them to turn over the prayer and spread glue around the edges of the paper.

Next, give each child a sheet of construction paper. Assist them in mounting the prayer onto the construction paper. This can be done with even margins; set at a jaunty angle; or so there are two very narrow margins at one corner and wide margins at the other. Have the children gently smooth the paper to secure the glue.

Hand out the stickers. Invite the children to decorate their posters.

Say: Take your poster home and hang it in your house. Have someone read it for you every day. Soon, you'll know more of the prayer. If you keep practicing, you will remember it all! Jesus gave us this prayer because he wants to teach us to pray.

Snacking With Pretzels:

Serve children pretzels in the traditional shape. Serve soft pretzels, if available.

Once again, show the children how to cross their arms pretzel-style, reminding them that this is how people folded their arms in prayer many years ago.

Say: This is your little reward for saying your prayers today.

Exploring Some More:

Invite the children to make Play Clay Pretzels.

Purchase the play clay or make your own.

Give out the play clay.

Ask: Does anyone know how to roll clay into a rope?

Have everyone practice rolling a rope of clay. Show how moving your hands along the growing rope keeps it from getting too thin in some places.

Put a real pretzel next to each child. Have the children study their pretzels. Then show them how to lift and place one end of the clay rope near the middle. Next, have them lift the other end and cross it over. It should look like a pretzel.

Say: I hope that when you see pretzels, you will remember that Jesus wants us to pray. He taught the disciples, and he teaches us, how to pray the Lord's Prayer.

If you are sending the Play Clay Pretzels home with the children, have them place their pretzels on paper plates.

Saying Goodbye:

Have the children hold their Lord's Prayer Posters.

Say: Put your poster up at home. Ask someone to practice the Lord's Prayer with you until you know it. You can pray this prayer your whole life. It's a prayer most churches use in Sunday worship. The whole congregation says the prayer together. That's part of sharing God's love at church. Goodbye, Lord's Prayer Pray-ers!

If you have decided to do so, send the Play Clay Pretzels home with the children.

TREASURE WORDS

Opening the Bible:

To introduce the message, tuck a paper heart into a Bible. Prepare by cutting out a heart shape from a piece of paper. Place the heart in the Bible.

Gather the children together. Hold up the Bible for all to see.

Say: Inside this Bible is a treasure.

Ask: What do you think a treasure is? (*gold and jewels, money, fancy things*)

Say: Most of us think of jewels and gold coins shining in a wooden chest when we hear the word "treasure." A treasure is a collection of riches, such as money and jewels. But a treasure is also a valuable person or thing. You are a treasure to your parents. They love you. You are a treasure of their hearts.

Pull out the paper heart.

Ask: What's this? (*a heart*)

Say: When your parent says, "I love you" or a friend says, "You're a great friend," you treasure those words in your heart. The words in the Bible are a treasure for our hearts, too, because they are God's words. In the Bible, these words become stories, poems, songs, laws, letters, prophecies, and teachings. We hear these treasured words when we come to Children's Church, Sunday school, worship, and Vacation Bible School. The church teaches us God's Word.

Sharing a Story:

This is the story of Josiah, the king who brought the people of Judah back to the Lord (2 Kings 22:1–23:3.) The children will follow your lead and respond with a thumbs up or a thumbs down sign. Practice this a few times and then begin.

Tell the Story:

This is a story about a boy who became king and how he brought God's Word to the people in his kingdom. Josiah was eight years old when he became the king of a land called Judah. He ruled from the city of Jerusalem and did what was right in the sight of the Lord. (thumbs up)

King Josiah walked in the way of his ancestor, King David, and he did not turn aside to the left or the right. (thumbs up)

When Josiah had been king for eighteen years, he called for his secretary, Shaphan (SHAY-fuhn). King Josiah asked Shaphan to visit the house of the Lord, which was falling down. (thumbs down)

There, Shaphan, the secretary, would speak to the high priest about repairing the house of the Lord. (thumbs up)

Shaphan told the high priest to take all the money from the offerings and to give it to the carpenters, the builders, and the masons so they could fix everything. (thumbs up)

While the repairs went on, the high priest found, in the church, a book of the Lord's laws. The priest gave the book to Shaphan the secretary to read. (thumbs up)

Shaphan gave King Josiah the good news about the work being done (thumbs up), and then he read the book of the law to the king. (thumbs up)

When King Josiah heard the words of the book, he became so upset that he cried and tore his clothes. (thumbs down) Once King Josiah heard all of the Lord's laws,

Supplies:
(for Opening the Bible)
paper
marker
NRSV Bible
scissors

he knew that he and all the people had been doing the wrong things (thumbs down) and not loving God in the right way (thumbs down).

King Josiah called together the high priest, the secretary, and others. He said, "The Lord must be angry with us because we have not been following the laws in the book! (thumbs down) Go and ask the Lord what we should do! (thumbs up)

The Lord sent a message to Josiah. The Lord was angry with the people of Judah, and their ancestors. (thumbs down) But the Lord was not angry with King Josiah (thumbs up) because Josiah was truly sad, cried, and tore his clothes when he read the Book of the Law. The Lord forgave King Josiah and the people. (thumbs up)

Soon King Josiah gathered all of the elders and all the priests and prophets, and all the people of Jerusalem and Judah together at the house of the Lord. (thumbs up) King Josiah stood before the people and read the book of God's laws. (thumbs up)

Then the king stood by a pillar, there at the house of the Lord, and promised the Lord that he and the people would follow the Lord's commandments, obey the Lord's laws, and love the Lord with all their hearts. (thumbs up)

Praying About God's Word:

Invite the children to clap twice after each phrase of the prayer, following your lead. Pray.

Exploring:

Send the children on a treasure hunt to find Scripture Treasure. Then they will use Treasure Detectors to find the treasure within the passages.

Before Children's Church, to create Scripture Treasure, print out the Scripture references for the passages below on separate strips of paper. (For example, write: "Psalm 44:21") Print enough so that each child can find at least one. (It's OK to print the same reference several times.) Use colored paper to make the clues more visible. Hide these references in locations where the children will be able to spot them.

To make a Treasure Detector for each child, you will need paper, scissors, tape, and drinking straws. Create each Treasure Detector by cutting out a paper heart and taping it to the end of a straw.

Say: In our story, a treasure was found in the house of the Lord while it was being repaired. It was not money, nor jewels.

Ask: What was it? (*the Book of the Law*)

Say: The Book of the Law was a treasure of God's words to teach Josiah and the people. Now you are going on a treasure hunt to find God's words! Look for Scripture Treasure, small pieces of paper hidden away.

Give the children any further clues they may need, such as the color of the paper.

As the children bring you the Scripture Treasure, hand out the Treasure Detectors. Ask everyone to sit down again.

Next, read the passages to the children. As you read, ask the group to wave their Treasure Detectors when they hear the words: HEART(S) or WORD(S). Emphasize these key words as you read:

Psalm 44:21: "For he knows the secrets of the HEART."

Deuteronomy 6:5-6: "You shall love the LORD your God with all your HEART, and with all your soul, and with all your might. Keep these WORDS that I am commanding you today in your HEART."

Psalm 51:10: "Create in me a clean HEART, O God, and put a new and right spirit within me."

52

Psalm 119:9-11: "How can young people keep their way pure? By guarding it according to your WORD. With my whole HEART I seek you; do not let me stray from your commandments. I treasure your WORD in my HEART."

Jeremiah 24:7: "I will give them a HEART to know that I am the LORD."

John 14:1: "Do not let your HEARTS be troubled. Believe in God, believe also in me."

Psalm 139:23: "Search me, O God, and know my HEART."

Matthew 6:19-21: "Do not store up for yourselves treasures on earth…but store up for yourselves treasure in heaven, where neither moth nor rust consumes and where thieves do not break in and steal. For where your treasure is, there your HEART will be also."

Say: You are great treasure hunters and treasure detectors! Remember, we are always on a treasure hunt for God's Word at church!

Snacking With Treasure:

Children will love decorating Treasure Cupcakes!

Invite the children to top the cupcakes with the alphabet cereal in honor of God's Word in the Bible and the candies to remind us that God's Word is our treasure.

Exploring Some More:

Let the children decorate simple Treasure Chests. Have the children select their jewels and arrange them in a design on their containers. You might need to do the gluing for the younger children.

Admire the finished treasure chests. Give each child a Scripture Treasure from the Exploring activity to keep in their chests.

Say: Today at church, you heard some of God's words. Your treasure chest will remind you of the treasure we have in God's words.

Saying Goodbye:

Have the children point the heart on their Treasure Detector toward their own hearts. Lead them in *saying together: I treasure your word in my heart.*

Say: One way we can share God's love at church is by learning God's Word and telling others about what we have learned. Goodbye, Treasure Hunters!

Send the Treasure Detectors home with the children and the Treasure Chests too, if they have made them.

Snack:

frosted cupcakes

alphabet cereal

colored sprinkles
gumdrops or
other candies

Supplies:

(for Exploring Some More)

disposable, plastic food storage containers

plastic jewels with flat backs and/or jewel stickers with adhesive backs

tacky craft glue

Message:

We welcome people to church.

Bible Verse:

"Whoever welcomes you welcomes me." (Matthew 10:40)

Supplies:

(for Opening the Bible)

paper

marker

NRSV Bible

scissors

Supplies:

(for Sharing a Story)

smiley face

WELCOME!

Opening the Bible:

To introduce the message, tuck a smiley face into a Bible. To prepare, draw two dots for eyes and a big smile onto a circle of paper. Place it in a Bible.

Gather the children together. Hold up the Bible for all to see.

Say: In the Bible, Jesus says, "Whoever welcomes you welcomes me."

Ask: What does it mean to welcome someone? (*to say "hi," to be friendly*)

Say: A welcome is an invitation to a place. At church, we welcome visitors to join us in worship and other activities. Jesus says that when we do this, it's the same as welcoming Jesus himself. It is important to Jesus that we make people feel welcome.

Pull out the smiley face.

Ask: What's this? (*a smiley face*)

Say: When we welcome someone, we need to use our best smiley faces! Let me see your welcoming smiles. (pause) Great! Another polite way to welcome someone is to shake hands. Let us practice shaking each other's right hands.

Demonstrate, and then invite the children to practice shaking hands with one another.

Say: A great way to share God's love at church is by welcoming people!

Sharing a Story:

The story takes children to a variety of church events where visitors are welcomed. As you narrate the story, hold up the smiley face used in the opening.

Tell the Story:

Let us pretend to go to activities at church to see what's going on. I hope there are visitors. If there are, we will call out "Welcome!" when I hold up the smiley face.

Practice this a few times and then begin.

On Friday evening, the youth group was meeting at church. The leader said friends were invited. Travis brought his friend, Connor; and Sarah brought her friend, Katy. The leader said, (hold up smiley face) "Welcome!" to all the visitors. After everyone arrived, the group played a fun, silly welcoming game. Soon all of the kids knew each other's names. They had a pizza party and all felt welcomed.

On Saturday, the church hosted a big supper. The church members brought dishes and baskets and trays of yummy food. They invited friends and neighbors. The pastor said, (show smiley face) "Welcome!" to all the guests as they walked in. Lots of other people also said, (show smiley face) "Welcome!" Afterwards, everyone watched a puppet show. The supper was fun. All the guests felt welcomed.

Sunday morning, people came to Sunday school. In the hallways, the church members said, (show smiley face) "Welcome!" In the nursery, parents said, (show smiley face) "Welcome!" In the classrooms, the teachers said, (show smiley face) "Welcome!" After classes, everyone went to Fellowship Time and said (show smiley face) "Welcome" to the new people. The visitors were glad to be there.

Before the worship service, greeters stood on the sidewalk, saying, "Hi! Nice to see you!" to all they knew and (show smiley face) "Welcome!" to all the visitors. When the worship service started, the pastor said, (show smiley face) "Welcome!"

During Children's Church, Matthew brought his cousin, Alden, with him. Alden was a little shy about meeting new people; but all of the kids were friendly to him and said, (show smiley face) "Welcome!" Alden said he would come again sometime.

On Tuesday evening, the kids' choir met to practice new songs. The choir director said she had a surprise. In came three kids who had decided to join the choir. They were smiling. The choir kids smiled back and said (show smiley face) "Welcome!"

Do you like to be welcomed when you visit a new place or join a new group of people? Remember, Jesus said, "Anyone who welcomes you, welcomes me."

Praying for Visitors:

Have everyone extend their right hands, as if ready to shake hands. Pray.

Exploring:

Make a Polka Dot Welcome Banner to use at an upcoming church event or to post in a classroom or hallway.

Before Children's Church using large, open, block letters, print "W-E-L-C-O-M-E" on the roll of paper, or print one letter on each sheet of paper.

Begin by laying the banner along a table or the floor. Set out the markers or crayons. Invite the group to color large and small polka dots on every letter. The varied size of the dots and their random spacing will add to the banner's charm.

Congratulate the children on their handiwork. Tell them when and where the banner will be used.

Say: This is a beautiful banner! Your Polka Dot Welcome Banner will welcome everyone who sees it.

Snacking With Smiles:

Create a smiley face snack. Decorate the crackers or cookies with smiley faces. You may do this ahead of time, or let the children decorate the snack themselves.

Exploring Some More:

Add a bit of bounce to the day with bouncy balls! To make Smiley Face Welcome Balls you will need inexpensive bouncy balls in any size, at least two per child, and a few permanent markers for drawing the faces on the balls. Bouncy balls can usually be found where party favors are sold, or in toy departments.

Begin by giving each child a single ball to decorate with a smiley face. Then invite everyone to gather in a circle and have fun bouncing the balls.

Say: Wow! Isn't it great to see those friendly Smiley Face Bouncy Balls! They look like they are welcoming one another to Children's Church. Let's bounce them some more! It's fun to welcome others to our church!

Next, give each child another ball or two to decorate. Explain that you will keep the balls on hand to give out as small welcome gifts to Children's Church visitors and newcomers.

Saying Goodbye:

Have the children look at the Polka Dot Welcome Banner and hold their Smiley Face Welcome Balls, if they decorated them.

Say: This week, remember to smile and greet the people who join us at church. Welcoming others is one way we can share God's love at church. Goodbye, Smiling Welcomers!

Prayer:
God of Love, help us to look for new people to meet and greet and welcome to our church. Amen.

Supplies:
(for Exploring)

roll of shelf paper or seven pieces of paper taped together to form a long banner

markers or crayons in a variety of colors

Snack:
round crackers and squirt cheese

or

round cookies and a frosting tube

Supplies:
(for Exploring Some More)

inexpensive bouncy balls in any size (2 per child)

permanent markers

Message:

The church teaches us about Jesus.

Bible Verse:

"So faith comes from what is heard, and what is heard comes through the word of Christ." (Romans 10:17)

Supplies:

(for Opening the Bible)

paper

marker

stapler or tape

NRSV Bible

scissors

Sharing a Story:

toy animal

extra helper (optional)

FAITH IN JESUS

Opening the Bible:

To introduce the message, tuck a paper cross inside a Bible. Make a cross by cutting, trimming, and taping or stapling two paper strips together. Place the cross at the beginning of the New Testament.

Gather the children together. Hold up the Bible for all to see.

Say: The Bible has two parts: the Old Testament in the front (show the children) and the New Testament toward the back (show the children).

Open the Bible to reveal the paper cross. Show the children that you have placed it at the beginning of the New Testament. Hold up the cross.

Ask: What is this? (*a cross*) Who died on the cross? (*Jesus*)

Say: Everything written in the Old Testament happened before Jesus was born. This part of the Bible tells us the history of God's people before God sent Jesus to the world. The New Testament tells us about Jesus and the early church. The New Testament is special to Christians because we believe in Jesus Christ. We want to learn all we can about him. The church is here to teach us!

Say the Bible verse for the children. Then lead them in saying it after you.

Sharing a Story:

Jesus was a teacher, a preacher, a miracle worker, a healer, King of the Jews, a friend, a Son, and a Savior. In this Q and A story, a toy animal (named Kelly) will ask questions about these roles of Jesus, and you will share some answers.

You may want to recruit a volunteer to be the voice and handler of Kelly or to pose the questions as you assist Kelly in answering. If you do not have a helper, use a silly voice for Kelly and move her about as you make the animal speak.

Tell the Story:

Say: This is my friend, Kelly Churchkin. Kelly has so many questions about Jesus that I invited her to join us. Would you like to hear Kelly's questions?

Kelly: Jesus sounds like a really smart guy. Was he a teacher?

Leader: Yes, Kelly. Jesus was a teacher. He liked to explain the Scriptures in the Old Testament. He wanted to help people understand how to love God and their neighbors. Jesus taught his disciples, travelers on the road, worshipers in the Temple, and the crowds that followed him.

Kelly: So, if Jesus was a teacher, could he also be a preacher?

Leader: Yes. When Jesus preached, crowds gathered around to hear him. He preached about God, the Holy Spirit, and the kingdom of heaven. Jesus tried to tell people the best way to live their lives on this earth. His "Sermon on the Mount" is famous.

Kelly: Someone told me that Jesus could work miracles, too. Is that true?

Leader: It is true, Kelly. Jesus worked many miracles! Here are a few: Jesus and his disciples were in a wild storm in their boat. The disciples were scared, so Jesus calmed the waves and stopped the storm!

Another time Jesus actually walked on water and his disciples saw him do it!

And one day a crowd of more than 5,000 people came to hear Jesus preach. All of those people were really hungry, so Jesus broke up a few loaves of bread and some fish. He blessed the food and, miraculously, that little lunch fed everyone!

Kelly: Wow! Awesome. Are there stories about Jesus healing people, too?

Leader: Jesus healed strangers and friends, grownups and children, rich and poor; and he even healed a woman who only touched his robe. He made blind people see. He helped the lame walk again. He healed people who had leprosy. Everywhere he went, families brought their sick relatives to Jesus.

Kelly: I sure wish I could have seen all those miracles!

Leader: Some followers hoped he would be the king of their country, but that is not what Jesus was supposed to do. He was a spiritual leader, not a ruler.

Kelly: Well, did he have any real friends?

Leader: Good question, Kelly. Yes, he did. He became very close friends with his disciples. Jesus called them his friends, and he loved them. And Jesus had other real friends, too, like Lazarus, Mary, and Martha. He used to go to their house and hang out.

Kelly: Did Jesus have a mom?

Leader: Yes, Jesus had a mother. Her name was Mary. An angel told her she would have a very special son.

Kelly: Someone said that God sent Jesus to us. Is that right?

Leader: Yes. God sent Jesus to us to be our Savior. Jesus asks us to believe in him, to follow him, and to be with him someday in heaven. He asks us to try to be the best Christians we can be. And if we ask forgiveness for the times we make mistakes and hurt others, then God will forgive us.

Kelly: And he wants us to forgive others, too.

Leader: Right! Jesus wants us to forgive others. Kelly, those were interesting questions! Thank you for coming to Children's Church today.

Praying About Jesus:

Ask the children to bow their heads. Pray the Prayer to Know Jesus.

Exploring:

Children will have fun playing the "Vine Line Game."

Say: In the New Testament Book of John, Jesus says, "I am the vine, you are the branches" (John 15:5). In the land where Jesus lived, there were grapes and grapevines that people saw all the time. So when Jesus said he was like a vine, they understood that he is the strong part of the plant, the vine that brings food, water, and life to the branches. When Jesus says that we are the branches, he means that we are a part of him and that we are joined to each other, too. Now you are going to make a Vine Line!

Choose a child to be the Vine. Tell the rest of the children that they are the branches. The Vine will *say: I am the vine, and you are the branches,* and then call someone's name. That child will become a branch extending one arm onto some part of the vine.

The Vine will again say the verse and call the name of another child. That child will attach to the first branch. The Vine will keep calling names until everyone is attached.

Play as time permits, inviting new children to take the part of the Vine.

The Prayer to Know Jesus:
God of Love,
the more we hear
about your
amazing Son,
Jesus,
the more we
believe in him.
Amen.

Snacks:

grapes
knife or scissors

photo of a
grapevine
(optional)

Supplies:

(for Exploring
Some More)

paper

chalk

bowls or cups with
a small amount
of water

Snacking on Grapes:

Follow the game with a refreshing snack of grapes. Wash grapes and then use a knife or scissors to create kid-size bunches. Cut the grapes in half for younger children.

You may want to locate a photograph of a grapevine in an encyclopedia, dictionary, or gardening book, or on the Internet, to show the children.

Exploring Some More:

Teach the children the technique of painting with wet chalk to create Wet Chalk Pictures.

Show children how to dip the chalk into the water before they use it to draw. Note how bright the chalk colors become when dipped in water. Suggest children create a collection of crosses or bunches of grapes, or paint a chalk portrait of Kelly, the toy animal who was today's honored guest.

Saying Goodbye:

Have the children each give Kelly a goodbye hug.

Say: One way to share God's love is by talking with others about Jesus. Tell someone what you learned about Jesus today in Children's Church. Goodbye, Followers of Jesus!

Let the children take their Wet Chalk Pictures Home, if they have made them.

CURIOUS CREATURES

Opening Your Hand:

To introduce the message, hold and cover a small toy animal or a picture of an animal in your hand.

Gather the children together. Open your hand to show them the animal.

Ask: Can you name this animal? What does it like to eat? Where is the best place for it to live? Does it make a sound? What makes this animal interesting?

Say: All of God's creatures are interesting, so it's good for us to be curious and to learn about the earth's creatures. The Bible tells us that God was very smart in creating them. Psalm 104 says: "In wisdom you have made them all; the earth is full of your creatures."

Ask: Are there creatures all around the earth? (*Yes*) Did God create food for these creatures? (*Yes*) Can you name some of your favorite animals? (*horses, penguins, monkeys*) How did you learn about these creatures? (*school, magazines, TV, the zoo*)

Say: I'm glad you like learning about the animals on God's earth!

Sharing a Story:

A favorite animal story in the Bible involves Noah, a boat, and pairs of creatures (Genesis 6:11–8:19). In this version, involve the children by leading them in simple hand motions.

Tell the Story:

You are going to help me tell a famous animal story by doing hand motions. Listen and follow!

One morning, as Noah nibbled some grapes, he heard a voice calling to him. He knew right away that it was not his son Shem or his son Ham or his son Japheth. The voice was God's voice! Noah dropped the bunch of grapes and said, "Yes, Lord?" God liked Noah because he was such a good man and right now, God needed a good man for an important job. As Noah listened, God said that a great flood was coming to cover the dry land. (cup one hand around ear)

God told Noah that he must build a huge boat measuring 300 cubits long. (stretch arms out wide from body)

And 50 cubits wide. (extend one arm, pointing forward)

And 30 cubits tall. (reach arm above head and wiggle fingers)

God explained that the boat must be made from sawed cypress wood boards. (make sawing motion with hand and arm)

Message:
We like learning about the animals on God's earth.

Bible Verse:
"In wisdom you have made them all; the earth is full of your creatures." (Psalm 104:24)

Supplies:
(for Opening Your Hand)

a small toy animal or picture of an animal

59

And there should be many rooms inside the boat. (make a fist and hammer)

And the inside and outside of the boat must be painted with pitch to keep the water out. (brush hand side to side)

God instructed Noah to build three decks. (Hold up 1, 2, 3 fingers.)

And make a roof to cover them. (hold hands together over head)

And put a door on one side. (draw a rectangle in the air with finger)

Then Noah called his three sons, and they sawed and hammered and painted until the boat was done. (sawing motion with hand and arm; make a fist and hammer; brush hand side to side)

God told Noah to go out into the land and take pairs of animals into his boat. So Noah brought two horses, two cows, two sheep, and two goats. (hold up 1,2, fingers--do this four times.)

And two cats, two dogs, two chickens, two ducks, two pigs, and two donkeys. (hold up 1, 2, fingers--do this six times)

God also told Noah to take pairs of birds. (wiggle fingers in air)

What other creatures did Noah take into the boat? (Invite the children to take turns naming animals, birds, bugs. Have everyone hold up two fingers each time a different creature is named.)

Finally, Noah and his wife, along with their three sons and their wives, boarded the boat. Everything was ready as God commanded. (two thumbs up)

It rained for 40 days and 40 nights. (Open fingers of both hands and close fists four times to show 40.)

Noah and his family and all of the animals and creatures were safe on the boat as they bobbed in the waters. (make a side by side wave motion with hands)

When the rain stopped and the flood waters dried up, it was time for every living thing to leave the boat! The End. (clap hands)

Praying About God's Creatures:

In honor of Noah's story, have the children line up in pairs for the prayer. Pray.

Exploring:

In this Talk to the Animals activity, the children will answer questions about what particular animals say, eat, and do. They will also draw animal habitats. Bags of animals may be available at many dollar stores and toy departments.

Begin by inviting each child to select a toy animal. In turn, ask each child to make the sound their animal makes (*cows moo, lions roar*); name the animal's favorite food (*monkeys eat bananas, tigers eat meat*); and tell what the animal likes to do (*horses run, hippos float in water*).

Next, hand out crayons and paper. Have the children draw the appropriate home for their animal. Suggest scenes such as farms, pastures, woods, ponds or barns for domestic animals; and jungles, grasslands, mountains, glacier ice, or deserts for wild animals.

When the homes are colored, ask the children to talk with their animal about the picture of the animal's home. Next, let them have fun placing the animals in the scene and playing with them. Tell the children they may take their animal and their scene home with them.

Prayer:
God of Love, we praise you for all the amazing animals you created. We thank you for saving the animals during the great flood. Amen.

Supplies:
(for Exploring)

1 or 2 bags of toy plastic animals

paper

crayons

Snacking and Learning:

Serve animal crackers! While the children munch, feed them a bit of information about an animal of your choice. For sources, check the children's section of the library, find a field guide, search the Internet, or locate a nature magazine.

Exploring Some More:

Play "All Aboard the Boat," using these options:

1. If you have access to a toy Noah's ark, arrange for the children to take turns loading pairs of animals. Someone can pretend to be Noah, welcoming the animals aboard.

2. Challenge the children to pair up their plastic toy animals. Fashion a make-shift boat from toy blocks, an upside-down grocery bag with a door cut into the side, or a cookie sheet topped with a construction paper tent. Let the children march the pairs into the boat.

3. Put the children into pairs, using matched slips of paper with animal names and/or simple drawings of animals. Have everyone draw a slip of paper and then find their match. When all are in pairs, you can act as Noah to call the pairs "on board" to a corner of the room. Have the children draw new slips of paper and play again.

Saying Goodbye:

Ask the children to hold their animals and animal home pictures.

Say: God's world is full of marvelous creatures. You are God's creatures too! Let's share God's love for nature by learning all about animals. Goodbye, Curious Creatures!

Supplies:

(for Exploring Some More)

toy Noah's ark with animals

pairs of plastic toy animals

grocery bag and scissors, toy blocks, or cookie sheet and construction paper

pairs of animal pictures or pairs of animals' names written on slips of paper

Message:

We are thankful for trees.

Bible Verse:

"Out of the ground the LORD God made to grow every tree that is pleasant to the sight and good for food." (Genesis 2:9)

Supplies:

(for Opening Your Hand)

tree leaf

marker

paper

scissors

GOD'S TREES

Opening Your Hand:

To introduce the message, hold and cover a tree leaf in your hand. To prepare, pick a leaf from any tree, or draw a familiar leaf shape onto paper and cut it out.

Gather the children together. Open you hand to show them the leaf.

Ask: What is this? (*a leaf*) Where does it come from? (*a tree*)

Say: This is a (type of leaf). Every type of tree has its own special leaves, bark, and shape. The Bible says: "Out of the ground the LORD God made to grow every tree that is pleasant to the sight and good for food" (Genesis 2:9).

Ask: Do you think trees are pretty? Which trees are the most beautiful to you? (*Maple trees because they turn red and orange in fall. Christmas trees because they smell good. The giant redwoods in California.*) Can you name trees that give fruit that is good to eat? (*apple, orange, cherry, avocado, banana, pecan*)

Say: Trees are an important part of nature. We need God's trees, and we are thankful for trees of every kind.

Sharing a Story:

Sing about why we need God's trees. The song is set to the tune of "When Johnny Comes Marching Home Again," also known as "The Ants Go Marching Two by Two." Invite the children to listen to the first line of every verse and then repeat it with you. Younger children may simply join in on the words, "Hoorah."

Tell the Story:

We need God's trees to use for wood. Hoorah! Hoorah!
We need God's trees to use for wood. Hoorah! Hoorah!
To build houses and chairs, fences and swings, bunk beds and tables,
And yo-yo's with strings,
And we all use wood from God's wonderful trees.

We need God's trees to give us food. Hoorah! Hoorah!
We need God's trees to give us food. Hoorah! Hoorah!
Apples and pears, plums and mangos,
Pecans and almonds and green avocados,
And we all like food from God's fruitful trees.

We need God's trees around the world. Hoorah! Hoorah!
We need God's trees around the world. Hoorah! Hoorah!
Using their leaves to clean the air,
Filtering the water with roots here and there,
And we need God's trees to clean the land and sky.

We need God's trees to have some fun. Hoorah! Hoorah!
We need God's trees to have some fun. Hoorah! Hoorah!
To climb and swing and sit in the shade,
Or play in the tree house we just made,
And we need God's trees when we play outdoors.

God's trees are really beautiful. Hoorah! Hoorah!
God's trees are really beautiful. Hoorah! Hoorah!
Colors and shapes, flowers and fruit,
Sweet smells from the branches to the root,
And we love the sight of God's amazing trees.

Ask: When we use God's trees for wood, what are some of the things people make? (*doors, toy blocks, birdhouses*)

Say: Thank you, God, for wood!

Ask: What is a favorite food that comes from trees? (*cherries, bananas, peaches*)

Say: Thank you, God, for the good food that comes from trees!

Ask: Do you like to breathe clean air and drink clean water? Did you know that trees around the world help us have clean air and water?

Say: Thank you, God, for helpful trees!

Ask: Is there a pretty tree in your neighborhood or schoolyard that you like to see? (*cottonwood trees in a row, a weeping willow by the pond, a dogwood in my yard*)

Say: Thank you, God, for making trees a part of our world. Let's all shout, "Hoorah!"

Praying About Trees:

Before Children's Church, pick a leaf for each child. Press the leaves in a book so they don't curl up as they dry. (In winter, remember the evergreens.)

Give each child a leaf to hold. Invite the children to look at their leaf as you pray. Pray the Tree Prayer.

Exploring:

To make Cedar Chip Sachets, bags are available at craft stores and wedding departments. Chips are available in pet stores and pet departments. If using netting or fabric, cut about nine-inch squares and twelve-inch lengths of yarn or ribbon.

Say: In Bible days, the cedar tree was an important tree The giant cedars of Lebanon were tall, around 120 feet, and also very wide, with trunks 40 to 50 feet around. The strong cedar wood was a favorite building lumber. Its beautiful, sweet-smelling wood was used in chests and for statues. Different types of cedar trees grow in America, and the wood-workers of today like to use cedar, too.

Set out the cedar chips.

Say: These are cedar chips. Today we are going to make Cedar Chip Sachets. You can use them to keep moths away from your clothes and to make your clothes smell good.

Bring out the sachet bags, or the fabric squares and yarn or ribbon. Instruct the children to fill the bags with cedar chips or to put a handful in the center of the square. Assist as needed to cinch the bags or tie up the squares. (It's best to double knot the yarn or ribbon.)

Say: I am so glad God gave us cedar trees!

Tell the children to put their Cedar Chip Sachet in a drawer or closet when they get home.

Snacking From Trees:

What's in season? What's on sale? Select fresh tree fruits. Wash and slice to create a delicious platter. If this isn't practical, purchase individual fruit cups of apple, peach, or pear.

As the children enjoy the snack, sing the second verse of the story song again (see page 62).

Tree Prayer:
God of Love,
thank you for
each leaf on every
single tree.
We love to learn
their shapes,
watch them dance
in the wind,
and see how they
shine in the sun.
Amen.

Supplies:
(for Exploring)

small sachet bags
or squares of
netting or fabric

lengths of yarn
or ribbon to
tie the squares

small bag of
cedar chips

Snack:

fresh tree fruits
that are in season
or
individual fruit
cups of apple,
peach, or pear
spoons

Exploring Some More:

Play "Be a Tree." Children will follow your direction to pose as various types of trees.

Group Poses:

Palm Tree: Have three to five children stand in a tight circle, back to back. Ask them to raise their arms above their heads. Explain that these are the palm tree branches. Ask them to sway their branches in an imaginary breeze.

Willow Tree: Using the same circle technique, have the children bend slightly at the waist, dangling arms side to side. Then have them sway the branches of the willow tree in an imaginary breeze.

Individual Poses:

Fruit Tree: Have the children stand with their arms outstretched and hands fisted. Pop fingers wide open to show flowers blooming, and then wiggle fingers to show growing fruit such as cherries.

Christmas Tree: Have the children first hold their arms shaped like a steeple over their head.

Say: Look how tall you Christmas trees are!

Then have them bring their arms down and angle them out from their sides.

Say: And your branches will look so beautiful decorated with ornaments!

Now invite the children to invent some new poses!

Saying Goodbye:

Have the children hold their Cedar Chip Sachets.

Say: Today we have smelled and tasted and thought about the goodness of God's trees. As you go out into the world, hug a tree and share God's love for nature by telling others about the wonders of trees. Goodbye, Tree Huggers!

ALL OF NATURE

Opening Your Hand:

To introduce the message, hold and cover a pretty nature picture in your hand. Use a photo you have taken, a postcard, magazine picture, or locate a picture online. You may need to fold or roll the picture to hide it in your hand.

Gather the children together. Open your hand to show them the picture.

Ask: What do you see in this picture? (*pine trees covered with snow, beautiful fish, fancy birds*) Where do you think this place might be? (*on top of a mountain, in the ocean, the rain forest*) What do you like best about the picture? (*The snow looks like lace. The fish have pretty colors. The birds look like they are having fun.*)

Say: Nature is all around us, no matter where we are. You can see more of nature when you are outside of town; but even in the middle of the biggest city, we feel the sun, wind, and snow. We see birds, trees, and clouds. We smell the rain and flowers. We hear dogs barking, thunder claps, and people talking.

Ask: What is something big in nature? (*the oceans, mountains, the sky*) What is something tiny? (*an ant, a drop of rain, a grain of sand*) What is something surprising? (*tadpoles becoming frogs, a volcano, a rainbow*) What is something pretty? (*a tulip, the sunset, fluffy clouds*) What is something powerful? (*an ocean wave, an earthquake, a blizzard*)

Say: Nature is a miracle that scientists are learning more about every day. The Bible tells us that God created the heavens and the earth and all that is within them. Nature gives us the food we eat, the building materials we use, and the water we need. We depend on the wool, cotton, linen, and silk cloth we wear as clothing; the fun and comfort of pets; and the beauty of the world around us. For all this, we praise God!

Sharing a Story:

Today's story is taken directly from Psalm 148. The children will participate by listening for the word "praise." When they hear "praise," they will pretend to be cheerleaders shaking pompons. Show them how to fan out their fingers and shake their hands to be the pompons. Choose a child who is a good listener to be the leader. Practice a few times, and then begin.

Tell the story:

This is Psalm 148.

> PRAISE the LORD!
> PRAISE the LORD from the heavens;
> PRAISE him in the heights!
> PRAISE him, all his angels;
> PRAISE him, all his host!
> PRAISE him, sun and moon;
> PRAISE him, all you shining stars!
> PRAISE him, you highest heavens,
> and you waters above the heavens!
>
> Let them PRAISE the name of the LORD,
> for he commanded and they were created.
> He established them forever and ever,
> he fixed their bounds, which cannot be passed.
> PRAISE the LORD from the earth,
> you sea monsters and all deeps,

Message:
We praise God for all of nature.

Bible Verse:
"Praise the LORD from the earth." (Psalm 148:7)

Supplies:
(for Opening Your Hand)

pretty nature picture

Sharing God's Love of Nature

Supplies:

(for Exploring)

(for Nature Mural)
shelf or craft paper

pencil

glitter glue tubes
or pens

markers and
crayons

(for Nature
Postcards)
index cards

glitter glue pens
or tubes

markers and
crayons

fire and hail, snow and frost,
stormy wind fulfilling his command!
Mountains and all hills,
fruit trees and all cedars!
Wild animals and all cattle,
creeping things and flying birds!

Kings of the earth and all peoples,
Princes and all rulers of the earth!
Young men and women alike,
old and young together!

Let them PRAISE the name of the LORD,
for his name alone is exalted;
his glory is above earth and heaven.
He has raised up a horn for his people,
PRAISE for all his faithful,
for the people of Israel who are close to him.
PRAISE the LORD!

Praying About God's Nature:

If practical, bring in an object or two from nature for each child to hold during the prayer and to take home.

Gather objects yourself such as flowers, pinecones, snips of herbs, or evergreen twigs. If this is not practical, craft and dollar stores sell packs of shells, river stones, and other natural objects.

Have the children hold the objects as you pray. During the prayer, fill in the name of the objects the children are holding, or ask them to do this. Pray.

Exploring:

Choose which suits your group best: a Nature Mural or Nature Postcards.

Nature Mural: If you cannot locate glitter glue tubes or pens, markers will be fine.

Before Children's Church, use a pencil to draw the outline of the skyscape and landscape for the mural along a length of paper. Begin at one side by drawing a mountain peak, which eventually becomes rolling hills. Have the hills soften into plains, then have the plains become the shoreline with a few lapping waves. Add simple coloring book style snowcaps, trees, and other features. Finish with a changing skyscape showing the sun over the mountains, clouds over the hills and plains, and the moon and stars on the shoreline. Trace over the drawing with glitter glue to add definition and sparkle. (Do not be afraid to draw a landscape. You can probably draw better than you think you can, and the children will not be overly critical of your work.) (Use markers if you do not have glitter glue.)

Nature Postcards: Before Children's Church, draw simple scenes on the cards, such as a mountain peak with the sun overhead; rolling hills and trees with a cloud above; or ocean waves meeting the shoreline with stars shining in the sky. Trace over the drawings with glitter glue or markers.

To begin the activity, set out the mural or postcards, and the crayons.

Ask: What do you see in these pictures? (*clouds, tree, mountain*) Are they part of nature? (*yes*) Can you think of other things that are part of nature to add as you color? (*flowers, birds, frogs*) Are we are part of nature, too? (*yes*)

66

Say: In Psalm 148, today's story, all of nature is called to praise the LORD, from the stars to the sea monsters to the people. When you pray, walk, swim, climb trees, and look out the window, take time to praise God.

Invite the children to color the mural or postcards. Hang the finished mural for all to appreciate, or send the postcards home with the children.

Snacking on Sun Bites:

To make Sun Bites, drain the pineapple and slice the bananas. Place one pineapple ring at each child's place. Next, have the children top their rings with a banana slice. Invite them to eat the snack with their fingers.

Say: Let's celebrate the sun with this sweet, sunny, yellow treat! They have a sunny name: Sun Bites! The sun's light and heat are important for the living things of nature. Hooray for sunshine!

Exploring Some More:

"Good Morning/Goodnight Nature Game." Divide the children into two teams. Position the teams opposite one another on the floor or across a table. Give one team a phrase to say as they roll the ball to the other team.

Next, give the other team a response to say as they roll the ball back. Team members will take turns rolling the ball. Here are some phrases and responses:

> Good morning Sun/Goodnight Moon
> Goodnight God/Good morning Earth
> Good morning Tall Trees/Goodnight Tiny Flowers
> Goodnight Giant Whales/Good morning Little Birds
> Good morning Green Alligators/Goodnight White Polar Bears

You and the children can make up more phrases and responses, as time permits, and repeat the above phrases several times, too.

Saying Goodbye:

Have the children look at the Nature Mural or pick up their Nature Postcards.

Say: Let us praise the Lord from the earth for all of nature! Every day, share God's love for nature by being good to the environment. Goodbye, God's Good Earth Lovers!

Snack:
pineapple rings and sliced bananas

Supplies:
(for Exploring Some More)

a small ball to roll

AWESOME CLOUDS

Message:

Clouds bring rain to the land.

Supplies:

(for Opening Your Hand)

a picture of a cloud, or a cloud shape cut from paper

Bible Verse:

"He [the Lord] will come to us like the showers, like the spring rains that water the earth." (Hosea 6:3)

Supplies:

(for Sharing a Story)

a stuffed animal

Opening Your Hand:

To introduce the message, hold and cover a picture or cut-out of a cloud. Gather the children together. Open your hand to show them the cloud.

Ask: What's this? (*a cloud*) What colors of clouds have you seen? (*white, pink, gray*) What comes down from gray clouds? (*rain, snow, sleet*) How do clouds move? (*The wind blows them.*) Do you know what happens when cool winds and warm winds bump against each other? (*storm clouds*) Do storm clouds sometimes make noise? (*booming thunder, crashing lightning*)

Say: Storms happen all around the world. We need them to bring water to the earth. Living things, from plants to people, need water. The rain and snow fill our rivers and streams, lakes and ponds, seas and oceans.

The Bible says that God is like a gentle cloud who "will come to us like the showers, like the spring rains that water the earth" (Hosea 6:3). Clouds bring life-giving water to the earth. God, like water, is life-giving.

Sharing a Story:

This story about clouds is told by an airplane pilot named Marty McCloud. Use a toy animal to play Marty. Speak for Marty and move the animal as she speaks.

Tell the Story:

Hi, my name is Marty McCloud, and I fly an airplane. In my years as a pilot, I have flown all over the country. Since I fly up in the sky, clouds are important to me. Every time I get into the pilot's seat, I wonder what kinds of clouds I will see. Clouds are a big part of the weather.

Before I start off down the runway, I must know about the weather at the airport I am flying out of, the weather at the airport I am flying into, and the weather in the sky in-between. Will I fly in blue skies with puffy little clouds and light winds? Or will there be big dark clouds in a gray sky with strong winds?

The weather affects how I will operate the airplane. Will I have crosswinds? Will a storm create downdrafts of wind? Will I have to land in heavy fog? Pilots pay careful attention to the sky and the clouds and the weather reports.

If you ask me, Marty McCloud, what I like most about flying, I'd have to say how wonderful it is to be up with the clouds. Did you know you can fly right through a cloud? It looks foggy on the inside. Flying next to a giant thundercloud is awesome. Pilots can fly airplanes above the clouds, below the clouds, or in the middle of them.

Of course, the earth looks very different from an airplane. It's like a crazy quilt of trees and fields, mountains and lakes, grasslands and seas. From my airplane, I can see where the clouds have brought too much rain. Flood waters make hilltops look like little islands, streets look like rivers, and houses look like boats on a lake.

Other times, I find places where the clouds need to bring rain. The rivers and lakes have shrunk; there is dust in the wind; and the fields and grasslands look dried up. The earth needs the water that clouds bring, but we can't tell a cloud where to go!

If I ever get tired of flying in the clouds, I might become a meteorologist. A meteorologist is a person who studies the atmosphere above the earth and studies the weather. Doesn't it sound like fun to have a job studying clouds? When I go to the library, I like to check out books on clouds and the weather—my very favorite part of nature. Well, it's time for me to say goodbye. The next time you see a cloud, think of me!

Praying About Clouds:

Have the children pretend that they are clouds, using their arms, hands, and upper bodies to create shapes. Encourage the children to say what sort of clouds they are (*fluffy, storm clouds, or filled with hail*), and then invite them to float about the room.

Then ask your "clouds" to freeze in place as you offer the prayer. Pray.

Exploring:

Children will have fun making Cotton Ball Clouds. Pour glue into several shallow bowls. Dilute the glue with some water.

Begin by giving each child a sheet of construction paper, a brush or cotton swab, and a handful of cotton balls. Place the bowls of glue within easy reach.

Invite the children to arrange their cotton balls into cloud shapes on their sheet of paper. When they are satisfied with their creations, they are to lift the cotton balls, one at a time, dab some glue on the spot, and then replace the cotton ball and press.

When the creations are complete, bring out Marty McCloud to listen to the children tell about their Cotton Ball Cloud pictures. Assist Marty in making happy comments about the children's artwork.

Snacking on Clouds:

Make sweet, fluffy clouds using real whipping cream or non-dairy whipped topping. Scoop the topping into bowls or paper cups. Try one or more of these mix-in options:

Fair Sky: Let the children shake blue decorative sugar crystals into the cloud fluff and mix in with a spoon. Explain that the sugar crystals are like water drops in clouds.

Storm Clouds: Let the children sprinkle cocoa powder to darken the cloud fluff. Then invite them to mix in hailstones of round, colored candy sprinkles.

Sunset Clouds: Let the children stir in a drop of yellow food coloring and a drop of red. Invite them to swirl the colors into the cloud to create lovely sunset clouds.

Children may eat their cloud treats with a spoon or with the help of a cookie, such as vanilla wafers or graham crackers.

Exploring Some More:

Let the children celebrate clouds with a game of "Cloud Hide and Seek."

Before Children's Church, tuck cotton balls, here, there, and everywhere around the room. Have the children hunt for the clouds. Invite them to count how many they find and report the number to the group. Then invite everyone to pile their cotton balls together to form a big, puffy cloud.

Play the game again, choosing one or several children to hide the clouds, while the rest of the group looks for clouds in the sky outside the window.

Saying Goodbye:

Have the children hold their Cotton Ball Cloud creations as you hold up Marty McCloud.

Have Marty, say: Look at all of your beautiful clouds! We celebrate clouds and the water they bring. We share God's love for nature's clouds. Goodbye, Cloud Watchers!

Prayer:
God of Love, thank you for your awesome clouds. The power and changeable shapes keep our eyes on the skies! Amen.

Supplies:
(for Exploring)

a stuffed animal

cotton balls (in pastel colors if available)

construction paper

diluted glue

shallow bowls

small brushes or cotton swabs

Snack:
whipping cream or non-dairy whipped topping

bowls or cups

spoons

blue decorative sugar crystals

cocoa powder and round, colored candy sprinkles

yellow and red food coloring

graham crackers or vanilla wafers

Supplies:
(Exploring More)

a stuffed animal

cotton balls

69

Bible Verse:

"Consider the lilies...even Solomon in all his glory was not clothed like one of these." (Matthew 6:28-29)

Supplies:

(for Sharing a Story)

plain paper plates
scissors
crayons

construction paper or tissue paper in a variety of colors
tape or stapler (optional)

FLOWER POWER

Opening Your Hand:

To introduce the message, hold and cover a flower in your hand. If possible, bring a real flower, since this will have the most appeal to the children and will best enforce the message. However, an artificial flower or a photo or drawing of a flower will do.

Gather the children together. Open your hand to show them the flower.

Ask: What's this? (*a flower*) Does this flower have a name? (*name of flower*) Do you have a favorite kind of flower? (*tulip, rose, water lily*) What do you like best about that flower? (*its smell, the colors, the shape; How soft it is.*)

Say: Flowers are beautiful. Seeing their lovely shapes and colors, smelling their perfume, and touching their soft petals makes us feel happy. Flowers are a wonderful part of nature.

In the Bible, Jesus talks about the beauty of the flowers. He says that even King Solomon in his fancy clothes did not look as lovely as the lilies do. God created the beauty of flowers. And God gave us many types of flowers to enjoy. Some trees have flowers, some grasses have flowers, some bushes and briars have flowers, lots of vegetable plants have flowers, and many wild plants from the mountains to the desert to the swamps have flowers. We plant flowers in our gardens. God brings beauty to the world through nature. Flowers are a part of that beauty!

Sharing a Story:

The children will participate in the story by pretending to be flowers. They will first make Flower Faces to wear. The children will then be divided into three groups. They will respond to the story by standing up and sitting down on cue.

To make Flower Faces: Before Children's Church, cut a circle out of the center of each paper plate, so the hole allows a child's eyes, nose, and mouth to show. The Flower Faces may be embellished with construction paper petals in pretty colors or with squares of tissue paper fan-folded and gathered on one side.

Have each child color his or her plate. If you have chosen to embellish the Flower Faces, tape or staple the paper petals or tissue paper fans around the plate rims.

When the Flower Faces are finished, have the children model them by holding them in front of their faces. Tell them they have now created a garden of beautiful flowers. Next, divide the children into three groups. Explain that when you point to a group, that group is to stand up and then sit down again. You will lead them in saying the refrain each time.

Tell the Story:

God created beauty, and we are beautiful flowers!
(Point to Group One.) **Some of us grow from bulbs.**
(Point to Group Two.) **Some of us grow from seeds.**
(Point to Group Three.) **Some of us grow from tubers.**

Refrain: *We are beautiful flowers!*

(Point to Group One.) **Some of us smell like perfume.**
(Point to Group Two.) **Some of us have stripes and dots.**
(Point to Group Three.) **Some of us have complicated shapes.**

Refrain: *God created beauty!*

(Point to Group One.) **Some of us like hot air and soil.**
(Point to Group Two.) **Some of us like cold air and soil.**
(Point to Group Three.) **Some of us like both.**

Refrain: We are beautiful flowers!

(Point to Group One.) **Some of us want dry air and soil.**
(Point to Group Two.) **Some of us want moist air and soil.**
(Point to Group Three.) **Some of us want something in-between.**

Refrain: God created beauty!

(Point to Group One.) **Some of us put roots in sand.**
(Point to Group Two.) **Some of us put roots in clay.**
(Point to Group Three.) **Some of us put roots in loam.**

Refrain: We are beautiful flowers!

(Point to Group One.) **Some of us live among rocks.**
(Point to Group Two.) **Some of us live in water.**
(Point to Group Three.) **Some of us hang in trees.**

Refrain: God created beauty!

(Point to Group One.) **Some of us make fruit.**
(Point to Group Two.) **Some of us make vegetables.**
(Point to Group Three) **Some of us make seeds.**

Refrain: We are beautiful flowers!

(Point to Group One.) **Some of us attract butterflies.**
(Point to Group Two.) **Some of us give pollen to bees.**
(Point to Group Three.) **Some of us feed the birds.**

Refrain: God created beauty!

(Point to Group One.) **Some of us go to the florist's shop.**
(Point to Group Two.) **Some of us stay home in your garden.**
(Point to Group Three.) **Some of us are harvested for tea and perfume.**

Refrain: We are beautiful flowers!

(Point to Group One.) **Some of us will surprise you at a party.**
(Point to Group Two.) **Some of us will show up at a wedding.**
(Point to Group Three.) **Some of us will visit the hospital.**

Refrain: God created beauty!

(Point to Group One.) **Some of us will become your favorites.**
(Point to Group Two.) **Some of us will be pressed in your Bible.**
(Point to Group Three.) **Some of us will remind you of your grandma.**

Refrain: We are beautiful flowers!

Praying About Flowers:

Have the children wear their Flower Faces. Ask them to stand like flowers with their faces tilted to the sun and one arm stretched out like a leaf. Pray the Flower Prayer.

Exploring:

Children will sculpt Play Clay Flowers. If you decide to send the flowers home with the children, you will also need paper plates.

Purchase the clay or make your own. Mix one cup flour, ½ cup salt, and two teaspoons cream of tartar. Add food coloring, one tablespoon of vegetable oil, and one cup water to the dry ingredients. Cook over medium heat for several minutes. Let cool and knead. Play clay stores well in air-tight containers.

Supplies:
(for Exploring)

Play Clay:
1 cup flour
1/2 cup salt
2 tsps. cream
of tartar
food coloring
1 Tablespoon
vegetable oil
1 cup water

paper plates
air-tight containers

cardboard tubes
from paper towels
scissors

Flower Prayer:
God of Love,
we share your
love for flowers.
Thank you for
their beauty in
the world.
Amen.

Cardboard tubes from paper towels can be cut into smaller two-inch sections. They are just right for cutting circles and flower petals. Press the end into play clay to create a small circle. If the tube is flattened into an oval shape, it creates an oblong petal when pressed into the clay.

Ask the children to think about the beauty of God's flowers, and then create their own. If they are going to take their creations home, have them put their flowers on a paper plate.

Snacking on Flowers:

Plan an easy Flower Tea Party! At home, brew, sweeten, and chill herbal tea made with flowers such as chamomile or rose hip. Look on the snack aisle of the grocery store for scallop-edged cookie rings, or decorate round sugar cookies with petals made of frosting.

Serve the tea and cookies, using flowered cups and plates, if practical.

While everyone enjoys the tea party, ask the children some questions about flowers:

Ask: What is your favorite flower color or fragrance? Do you have flowers growing at home? At school? At church? Have you ever planted flowers? What is the tallest flower you have ever seen? What is the smallest one you have seen?

Exploring Some More:

Play "Daisy, Daisy, Rose" with the children. Have everyone form a wide circle. Hold up the flower you used in the opening activity as you explain how the game is played.

You will begin as IT, since you have the flower. Tell the children that the flower (no matter what it looks like, is the "Rose.") Stepping out of the circle, walk around the outside **saying: Daisy, daisy, daisy, daisy** as you pass by the children. Finally, drop the rose behind a child, **saying: Rose!** and tap the child on the back. Explain that the child who is tagged is to chase you as you hurry back to your spot. If the child with the flower gets to your spot first, you are still IT. If not, the new IT walks around the circle *saying: Daisy, daisy, daisy, daisy!* until *saying: Rose!* while tagging someone else.

Play as time permits. If you are concerned with children running, ask them to walk quickly.

Saying Goodbye:

Have the children put on their Flower Faces.

Say: You are beautiful flowers! We are glad God created beauty in nature. We share God's love for the flowers of the world. Goodbye, Flower Children!

If you are sending the Play Clay Flowers home with the children, ask them to take these flowers, too.

BEE BLESSINGS

Opening Your Hand:

To introduce the message, hold and cover a toy bee or miniature bee.

Gather the children together. Open your hand to show them the bee.

Ask: What's this? (*a bee*) What sound does it make? (*buzz*) Where do bees look for food? (*in flowers*) What sweet food do bees make? (*honey*) Where do bees make their home? (*in a hive*)

Say: Bees are hardworking insects and are a very helpful part of nature.

Most fruits and vegetables begin as flowers. As the bees search for food, they visit these flowers. The bees roll out a long lower lip to reach into the middle of the flower to get sweet juice and powdery pollen. As the bees move from flower to flower, they also carry pollen on their fuzzy legs. The pollen from their legs mixes with the pollen in each flower. This causes the flower to grow, sometimes into fruits and vegetables.

Inside the beehive, the bees feed other workers and baby bees; and they build honeycombs, which they fill with honey. Bees are a blessing because they pollinate flowers that give us food and because they make wonderful, delicious honey.

Sharing a Story:

This story combines parts of Bible stories. You will read the story and lead the children in a chorus of *"Buzz-z-z"* after each mention of honey.

Ask: Do you think honey is a sweet treat? Have you ever tasted honey?

Say: We have lots of different sweet treats. In Bible days, honey was the most amazing sweet treat the people could imagine. Honey was valuable. We understand this when we read some Bible stories that mention honey.

Explain to the children that they are to listen for the word "honey" as you tell the story. When they hear it, they are to *say: Buzz-z-z.* Practice this, and then begin.

Tell the Story:

There was a time when the Israelites became slaves in Egypt. Many of them were treated badly. The people cried out with pain and sadness. God heard their cries and wanted to lead them out of Egypt. God chose Moses to take the Israelites to a different land, a good land, a land that had plenty of milk and HONEY! (Exodus 3:7-8)

All: *Buzz-z-z!*

As Moses took the people out of Egypt and into the wilderness, God helped them find good water, meat, manna, and in craggy rocks, HONEY! (Deuteronomy 32:13)

All: *Buzz-z-z!*

In the time of Jesus, there was a man named John the Baptist. John preached to people about their wrongdoings. If they said they wanted God's forgiveness, John dipped them into the river. John wore camel hair clothes and a leather belt. He wandered through the wilderness eating locusts and HONEY! (Matthew 3:1-6)

All: *Buzz-z-z!*

And those are Bible stories that talk about sweet honey.

Praying About Bees:

Invite the children to gather together and pretend they are huddling in a hive. Pray.

Message:
Bees are a blessing in nature.

Supplies:
(for Opening Your Hand)

a toy bee or miniature bee

Bible Verse:
"My child, eat honey, for it is good, and the drippings of the honeycomb are sweet to your taste." (Proverbs 24:13)

Prayer:
God of Love, thank you for honeybees who brought many blessings to the people of the Bible and the people of our times, too. Amen.

plastic spoons

yellow pompons
in half-inch and
one-inch sizes

googly eyes

black chenille
stems

colored paper
tacky craft glue

pairs of sturdy
scissors

Exploring:

Children will create Bee Buddies to play with. It's best to have an extra helper or two.

Make a sample Bee Buddy. Make a paper flower in the bowl of the spoon. Cut six oval-shaped flower petals. Put a thin layer of glue over the entire inside bowl of the spoon. Lay the petals so they meet in the middle of the spoon and fan outward. You may also cut a small paper circle in another color to place in the center of the flower.

To build the bee body, cut the chenille stems in half, so you have six-inch lengths. You will need four shortened stems for each bee.

Begin with the head. Place a dab of glue on the spoon handle, close to the flower. Press a half-inch pompon onto the glue. Next, create the bee's antennae by passing a shortened stem under the spoon handle directly beneath the pompom. Bring the stem ends up evenly on either side of the pompon, then twist together over the top middle of the pompon. Make sure the stem is snug against the handle and the pompon. Bend each stem head over the head toward the flower.

To complete the bee's body, put a dab of glue behind the head and press the one-inch pompom onto it. Use two shortened stems to create two sets of legs. This time, lay a stem across the pompom, bringing the ends down to twist below the spoon handle. Place the stems for the first and second set of legs near the middle of the pompon, but with some yellow showing between them. Make sure the stems are securely fastened, and then bend the stem ends to create the bee's knees.

Use a short stem to add wings. Pass the stem under the handle between the head and the body. Bring the ends up and twist close to the handle. Loop each end down toward the handle. Tuck the ends between the pompons.

To finish, glue googly eyes to the head.

Begin the activity by showing the children your Bee Buddy. Then, with the help of your assistants, go through each step as the children create their own. Allow the glue to dry before the children play with their Bee Buddy.

Snack:
slices of
honeycomb

or

honey straws

or

honey on bread
or crackers

Snacking on Honey:

Here are ways for children to get a taste of honey:

1) Serve slices of honeycomb. (Look for honeycomb in some jars of honey in grocery stores.) Tell the children to chew on the comb like gum, until the honey flavor is gone. Discard the beeswax.

2) Find honey straws (often sold for use in hot tea).

3) Let the children drizzle or squeeze honey onto bread or crackers.

Lead the children in saying the Bible verse before they enjoy their honey snack.

Exploring Some More:

Let children buzz around with their Bee Buddy. Gather everyone together in a spot designated as the "Hive." As Queen Bee, send out the bees in search of pretend flowers. Call the bees back to the hive after each search, **saying: Bees are a blessing! Come back to the hive, Bees!**

Saying Goodbye:

Have children hold up their Bee Buddy.

Say: Bees are a blessing because they pollinate fruits and vegetables, and they make delicious honey. We share God's love for bees. They are a beautiful part of nature. Goodbye, Bee Buddies! Buzz!

SURPRISING SAND

Opening Your Hand:

To introduce the message, hold and cover some grains of sand in your hand.

Gather the children. Open your hand to show them the sand.

Ask: What's this? Where have you seen sand? (*sandboxes, shores of seas or lakes*) What do you like to do when you play in the sand? (*make sandcastles, fill buckets*) Is the sand different when it is a bit wet? (*It can be molded. It holds a shape.*) What if it is really wet? (*It washes away.*) What if the sand is really dry? (*It pours like salt. It is easy to smooth out. It will not pile up very high.*)

Say: Sand is the tiny bits of rocks and shells that are worn away by wind and water. There is so much sand in the world that the Bible says it "can neither be measured nor numbered." Surprisingly, sand comes in many colors such as white, black, and pink, because rocks and shells come in those colors.

Although sand feels soft and smooth, it's not round. Sand has crystal-like edges. These edges can be sharp enough to sting you if the wind blows sand in your face.

Would it surprise you to know that sand is used to make mortar that holds bricks together? Or that sand is mixed with gravel and cement to make concrete?

A really big surprise is that sand can be melted to make glass!

Sharing a Story:

This story is based on the parable of the house built on the sand (Matthew 7:24-27). Start with an easy experiment with sand, rock, and water.

Place the rock in one pan and pile up the sand in the middle of the other pan. Fill the water container and have extra water on hand.

Gather the children around the pans. First let them take turns spraying/watering the rock until it is quite wet and water is standing in the pan. Refill the spray bottle if necessary, then let the children take turns spraying/watering the sand until it is saturated and dissolving into the standing water in the pan.

Say: You are going to hear a story Jesus told about a house built on rock and a house built on sand.

Invite the children to follow your actions as you tell the story.

Tell the Story:

In this story, Jesus wants us to understand the importance of being faithful followers.

Jesus says, "Everyone who hears these words of mine and acts on them is like a wise man..." (tap finger to temple)

Once upon a time a wise man (tap finger to temple)

Built his house (hammer fist against palm)

Upon a firm foundation of solid rock. (open hand, flattened palm with fingers held together)

The rains came down upon the house. (wiggle fingers from over head down to shoulders)

And the flood waters came and fell upon the house. (wave hands with palms down, from side to side)

And the stormy winds blew great gusts. (cup hands around mouth and blow out)

Afterward, the house built upon the rock was still standing. The wise man was safe. Jesus says that everyone who hears his words and does not act upon them is foolish.

Bible Verse:
"Yet the number of the people of Israel shall be like the sand of the sea, which can be neither measured nor numbered." (Hosea 1:10)

Supplies:
(for Opening Your Hand)
grains of sand

Supplies:
(for Sharing a Story)
2 pans
a fist-sized rock
2 cups of sand
a spray bottle or small watering can

A foolish man (thump heel of palm against temple)

Built his house (hammer fist against palm)

Upon a soft foundation of shifting sand. (open flattened palm with fingers wide apart)

The rains came down on the house (wiggle fingers from over head down)

And the flood waters came upon the house (wave hands with palms down, from side to side)

And the stormy winds blew great gusts. (cup hands around mouth and blow out)

Then the house built upon the sand slipped and slid (scuff feet from side to side)

Rattled and shook (shake shoulders and torso)

Broke and crashed. (shake open hands, then drop hands to sides)

The foolish man was not saved.

Our faith (hand over heart)

In the teachings of Jesus (form cross with fingers)

Puts us on solid rock (fist hand)

If we hear and act upon his words.

Now have the children look at the pans of rock and sand again. Ask them which they would choose to build their house on.

Say: When we follow the teachings of Jesus, we are building our faith on solid rock. This story helps us to understand the importance of being faithful followers of Jesus.

Praying About Sand:

If practical, give each child a pinch of sand to hold during the prayer. Pray. Then have the children brush their sand into one of the pans, and wash their hands.

Exploring:

Give each child a sheet of sandpaper, construction paper, and crayons.

Say: Pretend this sandpaper is a beach, sandbox, or desert. Draw a picture using the sandpaper as a beach, sandbox, or desert. What else would you include in your picture? (As an option you may wish to provide tiny shells, available from craft stores, to glue on.)

When the sand pictures are finished, invite the children to describe their pictures. Glue each picture to a sheet of construction paper. Hang their pictures up or send them home with the children.

Snacking on Sand:

Bury hidden treasures in a sandy treat! Purchase graham cracker crumbs to serve as pretend sand, and treasures such as chocolate chips. Layer the treasures into clear cups. Serve with spoons and invite the treasure hunters to dig into the desert.

Exploring Some More:

Place a large plastic bin, such as an under-bed storage box on a low table. Fill it with play sand. Place objects such as plastic cups, funnels, and spoons in it.

Give each child an object, or form small groups so children can share objects. Encourage them to play with the object, pretending they are in a sandy place.

Saying Goodbye:

Have the children hold their Sandpaper Pictures, if you are sending them home.

Say: We are glad to share God's love for nature, including surprising sand! As you go out today, look for the use of sand in our world. Goodbye, Sand Seekers!

GOOD NEIGHBORS

Opening a Shoebox House:

Decorate the lid of a shoebox to look like the front of a house. To introduce the message, place two small dolls or play figurines inside the box. If you do not have dolls or figurines, find photos of two people in a magazine, or make simple drawings. Give each person a name.

Gather the children together. Hold up the house.

Ask: What is this? (*a house*) Who lives in houses? (*people*)

Say: Let's see who lives inside this house.

Invite a child to take the lid off the house and bring out the people or the pictures.

Say: This is (name) who lives in the house. And this is (name.) They are visiting one another. They are neighbors.

Ask: Can you each tell me the name of one of your neighbors?

Say: It is nice to visit our neighbors and get to know them. God wants us to be good neighbors. Listen to this Bible verse: "Love does no wrong to a neighbor" (Romans 13:10). Remember, though, you must NEVER visit a neighbor without the permission of your mother, father, or caregiver.

Sharing a Story:

The story gives examples of good and bad neighbors. Explain to the children that when you **ask the question: Good neighbor?** they are to give a big wave and *call out: Yes!* if the person in the story is being a good neighbor. If the person is not being a good neighbor, they are to give the thumbs down sign and *shout: No!* Practice this a few times, and then begin.

Tell the Story:

When Mr. Trumble gave a happy toot on his horn, Colin waved and shouted, "Hi, Mr. Trumble!" Good neighbor? (big wave-Yes!)

Every time that Mrs. Gibble waves, Frankie never waves back. Good neighbor? (thumbs down-No!)

When Matt opened his candy bar, he tossed the wrapper onto Jackson's lawn. Good Neighbor? (thumbs down-No!)

When Tasha saw that the Morgan's dog had gotten loose, she asked her mom to call them. Good neighbor? (big wave-Yes!)

When Mrs. Ramirez broke her foot, Travis and his mom brought her homemade vegetable soup. Good Neighbor? (big wave-Yes!)

Message:
God wants us to be good neighbors in our communities.

Bible Verse:
"Love does no wrong to a neighbor." (Romans 13:10)

Supplies:
(for Opening a Shoebox House)

a shoebox
construction paper
markers or crayons
glue or tape

two small dolls or play figurines or photos of two people from a magazine

77

Prayer:

God of Love,
(children repeat),
every day,
(children repeat)
in lots of ways,
(children repeat)
help us to be
good neighbors!
(children repeat)
Amen.
(children repeat)

Supplies:

(for Exploring)
fluted paper
plates
yarn or ribbon
scissors
stapler
crayons
clear tape

When Amy and Aaron's grandpa died, Marco made them a card. Good neighbor? (big wave-Yes!)

When new kids moved in across the street, Lucy refused to let them come to her lawn and play in the sprinkler. Good neighbor? (thumbs down-No!)

When Rachel learned that Katelyn was moving away, she brought her a goodbye present. Good Neighbor?(big wave-Yes!)

When the boy next door needed to borrow Spencer's markers to finish a science project, Spencer said, "No way!" Good neighbor? (thumbs down- No!)

When they went to the neighborhood cookout, Jenny helped one of the dads open the ketchup bottles. Good neighbor? (big wave-Yes!)

When carolers came to their door, Lizzie clapped and said, "Great singing!" Good neighbor? (big wave-Yes!)

And....Are all of you good neighbors? (big wave-Yes!)

Praying About Neighbors:

Have the children form a circle and then link elbows. Ask them to repeat the prayer after you. Pray.

Exploring:

Children will decorate Good Neighbor Baskets.

Before Children's Church, cut paper plates in half, one per child and one for a sample. Also cut a length of yarn or ribbon about eighteen inches long for each basket.

Say: Years ago, the first day of May was called "May Day." On May Day, it was the custom to leave a basket on your neighbor's doorstep as a fun surprise. These baskets were called "May Baskets." They were filled with flowers, candy, or other treats. Today, we are going to make baskets. But we are not going to call them "May Baskets." We are going to call them "Good Neighbor Baskets." You can leave your basket as a surprise for one of your neighbors.

Let the children watch as you staple two paper plate halves together along the rounded sides, leaving the straight surface open, to form the basket. Staple a length

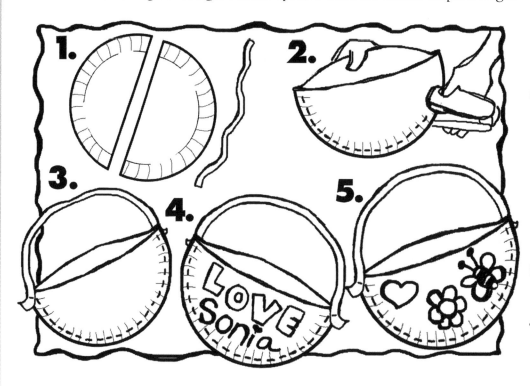

of yarn or ribbon to the ends of the basket to form a handle. Cover the sharp edges of the staples with clear tape.

Assist the children in assembling their baskets. Next, pass out crayons. Have the children write: "Love" and their name on one or both sides of their basket. Finally, invite them to decorate the baskets with hearts, flowers, bugs, and any other happy designs they would like.

When the baskets are finished, invite the children to hold them up for all to admire.

Ask: What surprises could you put into your Good Neighbor Basket? (*cookies, a card, candy, flowers, a tiny toy*)

Say: Your neighbor will be pleased to receive your beautiful Good Neighbor Basket.

Snacking With Picnic Foods:

Serve the children a food that neighbors might enjoy together at a picnic or cookout.

Say: Let's pretend we are all neighbors enjoying a fun picnic together!

As children enjoy the snack, invite them to tell about neighborhood gatherings they may have attended.

Exploring Some More:

Celebrate life in the community by inviting the children to take part in a Community Hop.

Before Children's Church, decorate squares of construction paper with simple symbols that represent places in a community: Library (book), Post Office (stamp), Church (church building with steeple), School (building with ABC's on it) and Park (slide or swing). You may want to add some other places, too.

To begin the activity, show the symbols to the children and ask what each one represents.

Next, tape each symbol to the floor, about two feet apart. (If your space is small, you may want to move to a larger space such as a hallway.)

Say: It's time to hop around our community!

Invite the children, one at a time to hop from place to place. As they do, call out the name of each place, **saying: Hop to the library, Maggie!** and **Hop to the post office, Maggie!**

Saying Goodbye:

Have the children hold their Good Neighbor Baskets.

Say: This week, let a grownup help you choose something fun to put in your Good Neighbor Basket and then go with you to deliver the basket to your neighbor.

Snack:
chips and dip
pretzels
fruit salad
or ice cream
and cones

Supplies:
(for Exploring Some More)

construction paper with simple symbols on them: book, stamp, church building with steeple, building with ABCs on it, swing or slide

masking tape

**Bible
Verse:**
"I do not cease to
give thanks for
you as I remember
you in
my prayers."
(Ephesians 1:16)

Supplies:
(for Opening a
Shoebox House)

construction paper

markers or crayons

glue or tape

a trash bag

toy bus

toothbrush

book

a shoebox

COMMUNITY HELPERS,
Thank You

Opening a Shoebox House:

Decorate the lid of a shoebox to look like the front of a house. To introduce the message, find three or four objects that represent community helpers. Here are some ideas: a trash bag for sanitation workers, a toy bus for bus drivers, a toothbrush for dentists and dental hygienists, and a book for librarians. Put the items into the box. Gather the children together. Hold up the house.

Say: Community helpers are people who work in our community. Today, we are going to talk about thanking our community helpers.

Bring out the objects one at a time. As you do, ask the children what type of community helper the object represents. Let them take turns sharing bits of information about community helpers they know such as "Ms. Josie is the crossing guard. She helps me cross the street when I go to school, and she is funny."

Say: God wants us to be happy, healthy, and safe in our communities. Community helpers make our lives better by the work they do. It is important to thank them.

Sharing a Story:

Children will enjoy solving these Community Helper Riddles. After they guess each riddle, lead them in saying an enthusiastic *thank-you* to those community helpers.

Tell the Story:

We stop people who are driving too fast.
We help children when they are lost.
We work hard to keep our community safe.
Who are we? (*policemen and women*)

Everyone: *Thank you, policemen and women!*

We weigh and measure you.
We take your temperature.
We write about you on the medical chart.
Who are we? (*nurses*)

Everyone: *Thank you, nurses!*

We ride on a big truck that is smelly sometimes.
We dump big cans into the truck.
We help keep the community neat and clean.
Who are we? (*sanitation workers*)

Everyone: *Thank you, sanitation workers!*

We read stories to kids.
We choose books for the community.
We help you check out books so you can read them.
Who are we? (*librarians*)

Everyone: *Thank you, librarians!*

We go from house to house.
We know who lives where.
We bring letters and packages.
Who are we? (*mail carriers*)

Everyone: *Thank you, mail carriers!*

We drive or ride in a great big truck.
Our truck has a very loud siren.
We use long hoses to put out fires.
Who are we? (*firemen and women*)

Everyone: *Thank you, firefighters!*

Say: Those are just some of the smart and caring people who help in our community. Thank you, community helpers!

Praying About Community Helpers:

Say: There is a verse in the Bible that talks about saying "thank you." Paul wrote, "I do not cease to give thanks for you as I remember you in my prayers" (Ephesians 1:16). Today, let's say "thank you" and remember our community helpers. (Pray.)

Exploring:

Many congregations have members who work as community helpers. Think about the community helpers in your congregation. Invite one to Children's Church to talk to the children about the work he or she does. If you do not have any community helpers in your church, recruit someone from outside your church. Encourage the community helper to bring along any tools or materials that relate to his or her job.

Say: Today, in honor of community helpers, we have a special visitor.

Introduce the community helper. Ask the children to please hold any questions until the community helper is finished speaking. Following the presentation, encourage questions. Thank the guest for coming.

A Snack From the Community:

Serve a snack that comes from your community. Consider local produce or a treat from a favorite bakery or restaurant. Talk with the children about where you bought the snack and the people who helped prepare and package it for you.

Exploring Some More:

Children will make Thank You Surprises for community helpers. Before Children's Church, decide where to deliver the Thank You Surprises so you can tell the children.

Make a sample Thank You Surprise. Write, "THANK YOU!" in bold letters on an envelope. Then decorate around the words with squiggles, dots, hearts, or other fanciful designs. Place two hard candies in the envelope and seal it.

Hold up the sample Thank You Surprise for the children to see.

Say: Inside this beautiful thank-you envelope are two delicious candies. Today we are going to make Thank You Surprises to give to community helpers.

Explain to the children where you will be taking the surprises. For example, "I am going to take the Thank You Surprises to the fire department. They will enjoy admiring the envelopes and eating the candies while they wait for the fire siren to sound."

Invite the children to create one or more Thank You Surprises.

Be sure to report back to them about the reaction you received when you delivered their Thank You Surprises.

Saying Goodbye:

Invite the children to close their eyes.

Say: Picture the face of a community helper you know. This week, if you see that community helper or any community helpers, *say an enthusiastic, "Thanks for helping us!"* What a great way to share God's love. Goodbye, Community Kids.

Prayer:
God of Love, thank you for the people who work hard to make our community a happy, healthy, and safe place. Amen.

Supplies:
(for Exploring)
community helper and his or her tools of the trade

Snack:
local products

Supplies:
(for Exploring Some More)
white envelopes
markers or crayons
individually wrapped hard candies

Sharing God's Love in Our Community

TEACHERS ARE IMPORTANT

Opening a Shoebox House:

Decorate the lid of a shoebox to look like the front of a house. To introduce the message, place an apple (real or decorative) into the box.

Gather the children together. Hold up the house.

Invite a child to come forward. Let the child open the box and pull out the apple.

Ask: What's this? (*an apple*)

Say: When we see apples, they make us think of teachers. In the olden days, kids often brought their teachers an apple as a present. Teachers were important members of the community then, and they are important in our community today, too.

Sharing a Story:

Bring a toy animal, named Izzy in the story, to help you today. Make up a silly voice for Izzy and move the animal about as you speak.

When the children hear a long pause, they are to fill in the missing rhyme. If children have trouble figuring out the rhyming answer, you may say it for them.

Tell the Story:

Hi! My name is Izzy. I am a (type of animal). And guess what! I go to kindergarten. Today, I'm going to tell you a rhyme about my kindergarten teacher, Mrs. Rice, and the things we do in her class. When I pause, you get to do something fun. You get to fill in the missing rhyme. Ready?

Say: I do something really cool,
    I am smart, I go to _____ *(school.)*
    My teacher's name is Mrs. Rice,
    She is really very _____ *(nice.)*
    She greets me in a happy way,
    When I arrive every _____ *(day.)*
    With Mrs. Rice, it's fun to look,
    At interesting picture _____ *(books.)*
    We paint and sing and play games,
    And she's taught us how to write our _____ *(names.)*
    We're learning to count, more and more,
    One, two, three, and _____ *(four.)*
    She claps her hands and praises me,
    When I say my A, B, _____ *(C's.)*
    I love my teacher! She is great!
    I'll see her tomorrow. I can't _____ *(wait.)*

If time permits, let Izzy lead the children in filling in the rhyming words another time or two. Then put the animal down.

Say: God wants us to listen to our teachers and to learn all that we can. There is a verse in the Bible that says, "My child, do not forget my teaching" (Proverbs 3:1). When you grow up, you will remember many of the things your teachers have taught you.

82

Next, ask each child to say the name of his or her teacher. If children do not go to daycare or school, ask them to say the name of their Sunday school teacher. If time permits, let the children also say something they especially like about their teachers.

Praying About Teachers:

Ask the children to close their eyes and picture the face of a teacher. Pray the Teacher Prayer.

Exploring:

Children will each decorate Apple Folders to give to their teachers. Before Children's Church, make a sample to show the children. Draw a large outline of an apple on a folder. Next tear red paper of choice, about the size of a half-dollar. Glue the paper pieces inside the apple outline. (It's fine to overlap or have spaces in-between the paper pieces.) When you are finished, use the crayon to give the apple a brown stem.

Before Children's Church, outline an apple onto a folder for each child. If you think your children might have trouble tearing the paper, you can do this ahead of time. If children are going to tear the paper themselves, cut it into six-inch squares to make for easier tearing.

Show children the Apple Folder.

Say: Teachers work hard. They have to keep a lot of papers. Sometimes they keep their papers in folders. Today, you're going to make a beautiful Apple Folder for your teacher. If you don't go to school yet, you can give the folder to another grownup.

Pass out the supplies. Demonstrate how to tear the paper pieces, if you have not torn the paper ahead of time. Explain to the children that they are to glue the pieces inside the apple outline, then add the stem with crayon. When the folders are finished, admire them before setting them aside to dry.

Snacking With Apples:

Serve an apple snack of choice.

Say: In honor of teachers, we're having an apple snack today.

As the children enjoy their snack, ask them if they would like to be teachers when they grow up. Then ask them what they think their favorite part of being a teacher would be.

Exploring Some More:

Set out some teaching tools that teachers use in the classroom. Divide the children into groups of three or four. Let them take turns being the teacher and the students as they use the items.

If this is not practical, bring in an activity book or coloring book. Tear out a sheet for each child. Let the children have fun using crayons and/or pencils to complete the sheets just as kids do in school!

Saying Goodbye:

Have the children pick up their Apple Folder.

Say: You have a beautiful Apple Folder to give to your teacher. *When you do, say: Thank you for being my teacher!* Teachers are important. We can share God's love by thanking our teachers. Goodbye, Good Students!

Supplies:
(for Exploring)
manila folders
red paper, such as:
red construction paper, computer paper,
red-patterned wallpaper or gift-wrapping
brown crayons
glue

Snack:
applesauce,
apple-flavored cereal,
apple slices,
or snack cakes with apple filling

Supplies:
(for Exploring Some More)
use several of the following:
flannelboard set,
flashcards,
ABC games,
picture books,
or puzzles
Bring in an activity book or coloring book.
crayons or pencils

83

Message:
In Bible times, people visited other communities.

Bible Verse:
"Joseph also went from the town of Nazareth in Galilee to Judea, to the city of David called Bethlehem." (Luke 2:4)

Supplies:
(for Opening a Shoebox House)
construction paper
markers or crayons
glue or tape
map

Opening a Shoebox House:

Decorate the lid of a shoebox to look like the front of a house. To introduce the message, find a map that shows your community and neighboring communities. If you do not have a local map, any road map will do. Place the map in the box.

Gather the children together. Hold up the house.

Say: In the house is something that helps us find the way to other communities.

Ask: Can you guess what it is? (*a map*)

Invite a child to take the lid off the box, discover the map, and hold it up.

Say: This map shows us communities and roads that lead from place to place.

If your community is on the map, point it out to the children. Then show them roads to other communities they may know. If you do not have a map of your area, point out several communities and the roads that connect them on the map you do have.

Say: It's fun to go to communities. Let's tell about a community we have visited.

If the children have trouble coming up with responses, **prompt them with questions such as: Do you ever go visit your grandparents in another community? Have you ever traveled to a fun place on vacation?**

Sharing a Story:

Children will learn an action rhyme to say when prompted during the story.

Say: In Bible times, people traveled to visit other communities, too. They did not have cars, trains, and planes like we do today. They traveled on foot and with the help of animals such as donkeys and camels. Today, we are going to talk about two people who traveled from their community in Nazareth to Bethlehem.

Ask: Do you know who those two famous Bible people are? (*Mary and Joseph*)

Say: Mary and Joseph needed to travel from their home in Nazareth to Bethlehem. The Emperor ordered all the people to return to their hometowns to have their names put on the records. Since Joseph was from the town of Bethlehem, that is where they went. That is why Jesus was born in Bethlehem.

Explain that you will pretend to be Joseph leading Mary on a donkey to Bethlehem. Since Joseph did not have a map, he will ask people he meets for directions. Every time you **ask: Is this the way to Bethlehem?** *the children are to respond:*

> *Up* (stand on tiptoes)
> *Down* (stoop down)
> *Where's that town?* (spin in a circle)
> *That way! That's the way to Bethlehem!* (point to the right)

Have the children stand. Practice leading them in the response several times. They will need to remain standing during the story.

Tell the Story:

I am Joseph. I'm traveling with my wife to Bethlehem. She is going to have a baby. Am I going in the right direction? Sir, is this the way to Bethlehem? (*response*)

Mary, I hope you are not too tired. Let me make sure we are still going the right way. Ma'am, is this the way to Bethlehem? (*response*)

I guess we will be there soon. Just to make sure, I will ask these shepherds. Excuse me, shepherds, is this the way to Bethlehem? (*response*)

There seem to be a lot of other people going in this direction too. Folks, pardon me, I just want to be certain. Is this the way to Bethlehem? (*response*)

It's certainly a dusty road, and I'm getting awfully tired. I bet you are getting tired, too, Mary. I hope this is the right way. Little girl, is this the way to Bethlehem? (*response*)

Mary, I think we're almost there. Son, is this the way to Bethlehem? (*response*)

Wonderful! We're here, Mary! We've traveled all this way and we're here, in the town of Bethlehem. I'm glad we were able to travel safely from our community to this one.

Praying About Traveling:

Say: In today's story, people helped Mary and Joseph by giving them directions. And when they got to Bethlehem, since all of the inns were full, a kind innkeeper let them sleep in his stable. That's where Jesus was born. God wants us to be kind to travelers and people who visit our community.

Ask the children to walk slowly in place during the prayer. Pray.

Exploring:

Children will make Bible Times Traveling Bags.

Make a sample traveling bag to show the children. Color a paper bag with bold stripes on both sides. Open the bag. Tuck another opened paper bag inside the decorated bag. Roll the top of the bags over an inch or two. Staple the length of yarn or ribbon to both sides of the folded rim. This will allow for the bag to remain open.

Say: In Bible times, people often carried their belongings in cloth bags. The cloth sometimes had a striped pattern. You're going to make a Bible Times Traveling Bag out of paper. With crayons, we'll make the paper look like beautiful striped fabric.

Show the children the sample. Once they have colored both sides of a paper bag, have them place another bag inside the decorated one. Assist them in doing this and in stapling on the yarn or ribbon handle. Ask them to model their bags.

Snacking With Traveling Bags:

Children will enjoy carrying a Bible times snack in their traveling bags.

Say: Today, let us have some Bible times fun. You are going to take a Bible times journey with a Bible times snack in your Bible Times Traveling Bag.

Explain to the children that cheese, crackers, and raisins were foods that travelers might have carried in Bible times. Give them each a snack to put into their bags.

If practical take the children on a short journey around the church. Point out pretend shepherds, cows, roads, and other travelers. Find a new place to enjoy the snack.

Say: This looks like an excellent place to pause on our journey and enjoy a snack.

Exploring Some More:

Mystery in the Stable (Abingdon Press, 2006, ISBN: 9780687493364), by Lisa Flinn and Barbara Younger, tells the story of two Bethlehem children who, from their rooftop perch, watch as travelers arrive in town for the census. When they see a young couple move into the stable across the street, the children set out to solve the mystery. If you can't find this book, look for another picture book that tells the story of Jesus' birth.

Saying Goodbye:

Have children put their Bible Times Traveling Bag on their shoulders.

Say: You can use your Bible Times Traveling Bag to carry things the next time you take a trip. Remember to share God's love by being kind to travelers who visit our community. Goodbye, Travelers!

Sharing God's Love in Our Community

Prayer:
God of Love, we pray that you will take care of people when they travel. Help us to be kind to travelers who visit our community. Amen.

Supplies:
(for Exploring)
2 lunch-size paper bags per child
36-inch length of yarn or ribbon (1 per child)
stapler
crayons

Snack:
pre-packaged cheese and crackers or raisins; or package small portions yourself

Supplies:
(for Exploring Some More)
Book: *Mystery in the Stable*, or any book of the story of Jesus' birth in Bethlehem

Message:
Our church is part of the community.

Bible Verse:
"The house that King Solomon built for the LORD was sixty cubits long, twenty cubits wide, and thirty cubits high."
(1 Kings 6:2)

Supplies:
(for Opening a Shoebox House)
construction paper
markers or crayons
glue or tape
picture of your church

Supplies:
(for Sharing a Story)
objects related to your church's history

Our Church Prayer:
Dear God, we are glad for our church building, and we are glad for the people who fill our church. Amen.

Opening a Shoebox House:

Decorate the lid of a shoebox to look like the front of a house. To introduce the message, find a picture of your church to place inside the box. Good sources of church photos or drawings might be the church directory, Sunday bulletin, postcards, or photos in a church album or on a bulletin board.

Gather the children together. Hold up the house.

Say: Today we are talking about another sort of house.

Open the box and take out the picture of your church.

Ask: What's this? (*a church*)

Say: That's right! In the Bible, the place where people worshiped was sometimes called "The House of the Lord." That's why I put the picture of our church in the box.

Ask: And what is the name of our church? (Have them repeat the name after you.)

Say: Our church is a member of the community. Today, we will learn about the history of our church and the part our church plays in the community.

Sharing a Story:

For today's story, tell a simple history of your church. Many churches have printed histories. The church directory is another good source of historical information.

The children will enjoy seeing photos as well as objects related to the history of your church such as Communion sets, Christmas decorations, or china plates with a picture of the church on it. Plan on telling a bit about the church in the community. Tell about events such as Christmas concerts, festivals, and mission projects.

Tell the Story:

In the Old Testament, there is a long description of the building of a Temple. Since the Jewish people didn't have a place to worship, King Solomon organized the building of a magnificent temple. The Bible says, "The house that King Solomon built for the Lord was sixty cubits long, twenty cubits wide, and thirty cubits high." The Temple was made of stone and decorated with carvings of fruit and gourds, beautiful statues, and a door covered with gold. Now let's hear a little bit about the building of our church.

(Give the children a brief history, and show them any visual aids that you have.)

Say: We welcome people in the community to come and worship here at our church (describe some of those events):
> when our church helps others in our community;
> when our church participates in local missions in our community.

Say: We're glad our church is a happy part of our community!

Praying About Our Church:

Teach the children this rhyme with hand motions:
> **Here is the church.** (hands folded with fingers tucked in)
> **Here is the steeple.** (pointer fingers form steeple)
> **Open the doors,** (thumbs apart)
> **And see all the people!** (open hands wide and wiggle fingers)
> Repeat the rhyme several times.

Next ask the children to fold their hands for prayer. Pray Our Church Prayer.

Exploring:

Children will make My Church Ornaments.

Before Children's Church, construct a church ornament for each child. Holding an index card vertically, make diagonal cuts at the top to form a roof peak.

To make doors, take a second card. Hold it vertically and cut in half across the horizontal. Place one of the halves over the bottom section of the church. Staple door hinges on both sides. Cut the doors apart up the middle. Cut a twelve-inch length of yarn for each church.

Say: Our church opens its doors to the community. We welcome visitors to our worship services and to our special events, too. Today, you're going to make a My Church Ornament. You may save the ornament for your Christmas tree, or hang it in your house as soon as you get home.

Give each child a paper church. First ask the children to open the doors and draw happy faces on the bottom half of the church. Say that these are worshipers.

Next, ask the children to draw a cross at the peak of the roof. Explain that most Christian churches display the cross, since the cross is a symbol of our faith.

Then invite the children to decorate the church any way they like. Finally, help each child staple a loop of yarn or ribbon to the top of the roof to form a hanger.

Snacking With a Church:

To make Frosting Churches: Decorate the churches ahead of time. Use the frosting to create an outline of a church with a steeple and door.

Say: These churches look good enough to eat! Let's!

As the children eat, encourage them to say what they like best about their church.

Exploring Some More:

Make Welcome Bookmarks to welcome people to your church.

A paper cutter makes this task easier. Children will decorate each bookmark with the symbol of the cross. Since this is a simple design, the children should be able to decorate plenty of bookmarks. The bookmarks can be placed inside hymnals or Bibles, given to worshipers as they arrive, or set out on a table.

Say: Let us make Welcome Bookmarks to welcome people to our church. We will decorate them with the symbol of our faith, the cross.

Coordinate distribution of the Welcome Bookmarks with the pastor.

Saying Goodbye:

Lead the children in another round of "Here Is the Church," then teach them the second verse:

> **Close the doors,** (thumbs together)
> **And hear them pray.** (hands, still folded, to ears)
> **Open the doors,** (thumbs apart)
> **And they all walk away** (take hands apart, make the fingers walk away)

Say: Today, as you walk away from our church, stop and look back. Say to your family, *"Look there's our church, a wonderful part of our community!"* We share God's love by welcoming others to our church. Goodbye, Churchgoers!

Make sure to send the My Church Ornaments home with the children.

Supplies:
(for Exploring)
plain 3-by-5 or 4-by-6 index cards
sturdy scissors
stapler
yarn or ribbon
markers or crayons

Snack:
graham crackers
tube of frosting

Supplies:
(for Exploring Some More)
markers or crayons
pre-cut bookmarks from craft departments, or cut your own

Message:
We help others in our community.

Verse:
"You shall love your neighbor as yourself."
(Leviticus 19:18)

Supplies:
(for Opening)
construction paper
markers or crayons
glue or tape
new socks

Supplies:
(for Sharing a Story)
large, clean sock
marker, paint pen, or felt pieces and glue

Helping Prayer:
God of Love, we are going to decorate posters for Sock Sunday. Everyone at our church will see our posters. On Sock Sunday, we hope that they will bring in nice, new socks to share with people who need them. Amen.

HELPING OTHERS

Opening a Shoebox House:

Decorate the lid of a shoebox to look like the front of a house.

Children are going to hear about and help organize Sock Sunday. This can be a mission project in which the children and others in the church bring in new socks to be donated to a local mission. Talk to your pastor or mission committee for support and approval of this project. Decide where you will donate the socks and on which Sunday the socks will be collected. Plan on promoting this project for a month or so before Sock Sunday.

To introduce Sock Sunday, put several socks inside the house. Festive socks, such as argyles or stripes, and socks in various sizes, will add to the fun.

Gather the children together. Hold up the house.

Ask: Who would like to open our house, reach your hand in without looking, and pull out what's inside? (Choose a child to do this.) Don't peek! I wonder what it could be! Oh my goodness! (Ask the child to hold up the socks.) What are those? (*socks*)

Say: We have socks in our house today because we are going to make posters for Sock Sunday, a day when we collect new socks at church. We will give these new socks to (say the name of the local mission and tell a bit about the work they do.) We will be helping people in our community who need clothes by giving them brand new socks to wear. What a great way to show God's love!

Sharing a Story:

Before Children's Church, make a simple sock puppet to help tell today's story. Find an old sock that is large enough to fit over your hand. Create a mouth that opens and closes by pushing in the toe of the sock between your thumb and fingers. Use a marker, paint pen, or felt and glue to make the puppet's eyes and a nose on the top, and a tongue inside its mouth. Consider using felt to create hair or a hat. Keep the puppet hidden until it is time to tell the story, then put it on your hand.

Tell the Story:

Hi! My name is Sidney the Sock. Since I am an old sock, I got turned into a sock puppet. Maybe you can make a puppet like me with one of your old socks!

I know there are kids and grownups who cannot afford to buy their own socks. Imagine how happy they will be to receive brand new socks! Sock Sunday is a wonderful way to help others. You kids are really loving kids to help with such an important project. I heard you are going to decorate really cool posters!

I would love to take a turn meeting each of you. When it is your turn to hold me, tell me your name and your favorite color of socks.

Let each child take a turn with Sidney the Sock. When the children are finished, put Sidney back on your own hand. Say your name and your favorite color sock, then let Sidney announce that he is going to take a little nap.

Praying About Helping:

Say: There is a verse in the Bible that talks about loving other people: "You shall love your neighbor as yourself" (Leviticus 19:18). This means that we should treat other people as we want to be treated. Since we like to have new, clean socks, God wants us to give them to others, too. Let's say a prayer about Sock Sunday. (Pray.)

Exploring:

Children will decorate posters for Sock Sunday. Plan on two to four children working on each poster.

Before Children's Church, in the center of each sheet of posterboard, use a marker to write:

> SOCK SUNDAY
> (Date)
> PLEASE BRING DONATIONS
> OF NEW SOCKS, ANY SIZE,
> TO HELP OTHERS
> IN OUR COMMUNITY.

Use the marker to outline the shapes of socks for the children to color. On each poster, as an example, color in one of the socks using bright colors and a design such as stripes or polka dots.

To begin the activity, hold up one of the posters.

Say: This is a poster to tell people about Sock Sunday.

Read the poster to the children.

Say: But look at all those plain socks. We need to decorate them!

Set out the posters for the children to decorate. While they work, let Sidney the Sock watch them and make encouraging comments such as "Those are the coolest socks I have seen in a long time" and "Gosh, I would love to be one of those socks." When the posters are finished, hold them up for all to admire.

Say: We will hang these posters in our church so everyone can learn about Sock Sunday. The socks we collect will help people who need them.

About a month before Sock Sunday, hang the posters. Arrange to have Sock Sunday announced at the worship service for several weeks prior to the collection date. (Consider letting Sydney the Sock help with the announcements.) Place a notice in the bulletin and/or newsletter explaining Sock Sunday.

On Sock Sunday, set out baskets to hold the socks. As people come into the church, they can drop their sock donations into the baskets. If practical, ask two or three children to stand nearby to thank people for their donations. Leave the baskets in the church for a few more Sundays, and then deliver the socks to the mission organization.

Snacking With Canned Fruit:

Along with clothing, many shelters welcome donations of canned goods. Serve canned fruit to help the children understand the need for food donations in your community.

When you drain the juice from the fruit, rinse off a can to show the children.

Hold up the fruit can.

Say: In our community, just as there are people who need clothes, there are also people who are hungry and who need food. Our delicious snack came from a can. One of the ways that we can help hungry people is with donations of canned goods. (You might want to say more about how your church helps the hungry in your community.)

Serve the fruit. Let Sydney the Sock tease the children by asking for a taste of their snack.

Supplies:
(for Exploring)

sheets of posterboard

a bold marker for writing

crayons

(for Sock Sunday)

several baskets for collecting the socks

Snack:
canned fruit
spoons and
bowls or cups

89

Exploring Some More:

To play "Sock, Sock, Whose Got the Sock?" you will need a sock. Choose a child to be the Guesser. The Guesser will stand in the center of the circle. Have the rest of the children form a tight circle around the Guesser. (Shoulders should be touching.)

Tell the children to put their hands behind their backs. Explain that they are to pass the sock around the circle. In order to confuse the guesser, everyone should pretend they are passing the sock at the same time. The sock may be passed in either direction and passers may switch directions at any time.

While this is being done, everyone *calls out together: Sock, sock, whose got the sock?* over and over again. When you **call: Stop!** the Guesser must guess who has the sock.

Give the sock to one of the children to begin the game. After a while, **call out: Stop!** Let the Guesser take a guess at who has the sock.

Have the child with the sock hold it up. Choose a new Guesser and play again.

If you have less than six children, it will be difficult to make a tight circle. Instead, you might want to line the children up, with the Guesser facing them.

Saying Goodbye:

Put on Sidney the Sock.

Say: We can share God's love by helping those in our community who need clothes and food. Thanks for making Sock Sunday posters. If you go shopping with your parents this week, ask them to help you pick out socks to donate on Sock Sunday. Goodbye, Helpers!

Let Sidney the Sock give each child a goodbye kiss.

JESUS VISITED COMMUNITIES

Opening a Shoebox House:

Using construction paper, markers or crayons, and glue or tape, decorate the lid of a shoebox to look like the front of a house. Put a paper cup inside the house.

Gather the children together. Hold up the house. Invite a child to come forward, open the box, and take out the cup.

Ask: What's this? (*a paper cup*) If I wanted to fill this paper cup with water, where would I get the water? (*from the faucet, at the sink, from a bottle of water, from the drinking fountain*)

Say: Nowadays, when people want water, it is easy to find. But in Jesus' time, when people wanted water, they usually had to go to a well or stream. In today's Bible story, Jesus visits a community well for a drink of water.

Sharing a Story:

Children will hear the story of Jesus talking with the woman at the well. After the story, they will take turns serving one another drinks of water from a pretend well.

A new, washed plastic bucket or a large cooking pot can serve as the well. You will also need a long ladle and paper cups. Before the story begins, fill the well with water and have the ladle and cups nearby.

Tell the Story:

Jesus traveled from community to community sharing the good news of God's love.

One day Jesus went to a city called Sychar (SIGH-kahr). Jesus was tired from traveling. He sat down by a well. A woman came up to him, and Jesus said, "Give me a drink." She was surprised that he asked her for a drink because she was a Samaritan and he was Jewish. Usually the Jewish people did not share things with the Samaritans.

As he talked with her, Jesus helped the Samaritan woman understand that he was the Messiah, the Son of God. Jesus showed her love. By visiting communities like this one, Jesus was able to help people understand that he was God's Son and that he was sent by God to tell them about God's love.

Sometimes, when people are thirsty, we show we care for them by bringing them a drink of water. Today, in honor of Jesus and the Samaritan woman at the well, let's serve one another drinks from our pretend well.

Let the children come forward, one a time, ladle some water in a cup, and offer it to another child. That child will then come forward and serve the next cup of water. Continue until all the children have been served. Let the last child serve you.

Say: Wasn't that delicious water! And wasn't it nice to offer it to one another!

Praying About Jesus:

Say: Jesus traveled from community to community, sharing the news of God's love. Jesus has gone to be with God, so he will not visit our community in person. But we remember him here at our church and as we live our lives. (Pray.)

Message:
Jesus shared God's love in communities.

Verse:
"A Samaritan woman came to draw water, and Jesus said to her, 'Give me a drink.'" (John 4:7)

Supplies:
(for Opening a Shoebox House)
construction paper
markers or crayons
glue or tape
paper cup

Supplies:
(for Sharing a Story)
new, clean bucket or cooking pot
paper cups
long ladle
water

Prayer:
God of Love, thank you for sending Jesus from community to community. We're glad we can read the stories of the people he met and the lessons he taught them. Amen.

91

Supplies:

(for Exploring)

lunch-size
paper bags

scissors

crayons

Exploring:

Make a Bible House. Before Children's Church, cut paper bags in half across the width, one per child. (Recycle the rest of the paper bag.) Cut an upside-down "L" shape into the front of the bag to create a door. Flatten the bag for easy coloring. Make a sample, by adding front and back windows, to show to the children.

Hold up the sample Bible House.

Say: When Jesus traveled to a community, he often visited people in their homes. In Bible times, many of the houses were made of mud, bricks, or stone. The roofs of these houses were usually flat. Homeowners used the roof to dry their laundry as well as to dry fresh fruit such as raisins and dates. In hot weather, the people sometimes even slept on their roofs.

Ask: Do you think it would be fun to sleep on your roof? Do you think your parents would let you sleep on the roof?

Say: Let's make our own Bible Houses with flat roofs. You may take your house home to remind you that Jesus visited people in their communities.

Have children color their houses. When they are finished, show them how to open their houses so that they will stand up. If time permits, they may enjoy putting their houses next to one another to create Bible villages.

Snacking:

Help children understand that raisins are dried grapes. Wash the grapes and cut them in half for the younger children, and into small bunches for the older ones. Serve individual boxes of raisins (or a small serving of raisins), along with the grapes.

Say: In Bible times, people sometimes dried fruit on the roof of their houses. Look at the grapes. Now look at the raisins. It is almost hard to believe they are the same fruit. But that is what happens when fruit is dried. It shrivels up. Dried fruits such as raisins last a long time. This was good, since in Bible times they didn't have refrigerators or freezers.

Serve the snack. Ask children which they prefer: grapes or raisins.

Exploring Some More:

In honor of today's Bible story, children can decorate My Very Own Water Bottle. You'll need a small bottle of water for each child, adhesive mailing labels or name-tags, permanent markers, and colorful stickers.

Ask: What did Jesus ask for in today's Bible story? (*a drink of water*)

Say: Jesus was thirsty. We get thirsty too! Today, you're going to create My Very Own Water Bottle. You can open the bottle and drink the water. When that water is gone, you can fill your bottle with more water whenever you want.

Have the children print their first name on a label or nametag. (You may need to assist those who cannot write their names yet.) Have them peel the backing off the label and place the label on the center of the bottle on top of the manufacturer's label. Next, invite the children to decorate the rest of their bottle with colorful stickers.

Supplies:

(Exploring Some
More)

adhesive mailing
labels or nametags

small bottles of
water

colorful stickers

crayons

Saying Goodbye:

Ask the children to pick up their Bible Houses and their water bottles if they have decorated those, too.

Say: Jesus visited people in communities to tell them the good news of God's love. You can do that too! As your family talks with people in our community, invite them to church. That's a great way to share God's love. Goodbye, Friends of Jesus!

GOD CREATED PEOPLE

Opening a Newspaper:

Use photos of people in the newspaper to introduce today's message. Plan on showing these photos to the children, with a word of explanation such as: These are Boy Scouts who raised money for people who are homeless; This man lives in Africa; and This woman won an award for her paintings.

Gather the children together. Hold up the newspaper.

Ask: What's this? (*a newspaper*)

Say: Let's open this newspaper to see if we can find pictures of people.

Point out the photos.

Say: It is interesting to look in the newspaper and see pictures of people who live in God's world. God created the world and all the people who live here.

Sharing a Story:

Children will decorate a Paper Plate Face to wave during the story. Make a sample to show the children. Draw a simple, cheerful face on a plate. Give the face a skin tone that reflects one of the many shades of human skin.

To begin, hold up the Paper Plate Face.

Say: We are glad that God created people! Let's make some Paper Plate Faces to wave during today's story.

Give each child a paper plate. Set out the crayons. Remind the children that people come in a variety of skin tones. Encourage them to color their paper plate faces in one of those skin tones. When the faces are finished, ask everyone to wave them in the air at the same time.

Say: Hooray for all God's people! During the story, when I hold up my Paper Plate Face, you are to hold up yours, too, and *say: Hooray for God's people.*

Practice this a few times, then begin the story.

Tell the Story:

God created Franz, who lives in Germany. (hold up face)

All: Hooray for God's people!

God created Jessica, who lives in the United States. (hold up face)

All: Hooray for God's people!

God created Ramia, who lives in Egypt. (hold up face)

All: Hooray for God's people!

Message:
God created the
world and
its people.

Bible Verse:
"In the image of
God he created
them; male and
female he
created them."
(Genesis 1:27)

Supplies:
(Opening a
Newspaper)
newspaper

Supplies:
(for Sharing a Story)
plain paper plates
crayons

93

God created Miguel, who lives in Mexico. (hold up face)

All: Hooray for God's people!

God created Jelani, who lives in Kenya. (hold up face)

All: Hooray for God's people!

God created Yumiko, who lives in Japan. (hold up face)

All: Hooray for God's people!

God created Tim, who lives in Canada. (hold up face)

All: Hooray for God's people!

God created Snofrid, who lives in Sweden. (hold up face)

All: Hooray for God's people!

God created Kim, who lives in Korea. (hold up face)

All: Hooray for God's people!

God created Rosa, who lives in Brazil. (hold up face)

All: Hooray for God's people!

God create James, who lives in Israel. (hold up face)

All: Hooray for God's people!

God created Shantah, who lives in India. (hold up face)

All: Hooray for God's people!

God created Marie Clare, who lives in France. (hold up face)

All: Hooray for God's people!

One of the ways that we can share God's love with others is by honoring all of God's people and shouting "Hooray!"

Praying About People:

Read the Bible verse, Genesis 1:27, to the children.

Say: We are glad that God created people. Let us hug our Paper Plate Face as we say a prayer.

Show the children how to hold their paper plate face to their chest and cross their arms over it. Pray the People Prayer.

Exploring:

Play two fun games in celebration of the world's people:

People Roll:

Have the children sit or stand in a circle.

Say: We're glad that God filled the world with people.

Hold up the ball.

Say: Let us pretend that this ball is the world. When the ball comes to you, pick it up and say the name of a person you know. Then roll it to someone else.

Play the game until everyone has had at least one turn to name a person.

People Hop:

Have the children stand in a wide circle.

Say: Let us pretend this circle is the world. And let us play "People Hop!" Listen carefully and hop the way I tell you:

People Prayer:

God of Love, we are glad that you filled the earth with wonderful people. Thank you! Amen.

Supplies:

(for Exploring)

large ball

Let's hop forward three times for all the people who live where it is cold.

Now let's hop back three times for all the people who live where it's hot.

Now let's hop on one foot three times for all the people who live near us.

Now let's hop on the other foot three times for the people who live far away.

Now let's hop forward three times for all the girls and women in the world.

Now let's hop back three times for all the boys and men in the world.

Now let's hop on one foot three times for all the children in the world.

Now let's hop on the other foot three times for all the grownups in the world.

Now let's hop forward three times for all the teenagers in the world.

Now let's hop back three times for all the grandmas and grandpas in the world.

Now let's hop on one foot three times for everyone at our church.

Now let's hop on the other foot three times for everyone in our community.

Now let's hop on both feet three times for all the people in the world.

Snacking With a People Cookie-Cake:

To create a People Cookie-Cake: Preheat the oven to 350 degrees. Line a cookie sheet with aluminum foil. Press the dough onto the foil to form a large circle. Bake the cake until lightly browned. (Watch carefully as cookie-cakes burn easily.) When the cake is cooled, use the frosting to draw a simple smiley face.

Bring out the cake.

Say: This round cake represents God's world and all of the world's people! It's a People Cookie-Cake!

Use a knife to cut the cake into small pieces.

Exploring Some More:

Lead the children in a discussion of God's wonderful creation: people.

Say: We are glad that God made people. And we are glad that God gave people wonderful senses to help us live.

Ask: Can you name the five senses? *(sight, hearing, taste, touch, smell)*

Ask the following questions, inviting each child to answer:

What is most amazing thing you have ever seen?

What is the best sound you have ever heard?

What is the most delicious food you have ever tasted?

What is the softest thing you have ever touched?

What is the strangest thing you have ever smelled?

Saying Goodbye:

Have the children hug their Paper Plate Face again.

Say: Just for fun, when you get home, give your Paper Plate Face a name. Keep your face in your room to remind you that God created wonderful people. God wants us to show our love to the people of the world. Goodbye, Kids of the World!

Snack:
roll of cookie dough

tube of frosting

aluminum foil

round baking sheet or cookie sheet

potholders

oven

knife

CHRISTIANS EVERYWHERE!

Opening a Newspaper:

Message:

There are Christian churches all over the world.

Bible Verse:

"Go therefore and make disciples of all nations." (Matthew 28:19)

Supplies:

(Opening a Newspaper)

paper

scissors

newspaper

tape

crayon

Introduce the message by cutting out a large paper cross and taping it to one of the pages of a section of newspaper, or color a cross onto a page of the newspaper.

Gather the children together. Hold up the newspaper.

Say: Inside this newspaper is the most important symbol of the Christian church.

Ask: Can anyone guess what that symbol is? (*a cross*) Can we find one?

Let the children watch as you turn the pages of the paper until you reach the cross.

Say: There are Christian churches all over the world. Almost every Christian church has a cross on the outside of the building, inside the building, or in both places. Today, we are going to take a pretend world tour to visit some of those churches.

Sharing a Story:

You will take the children on a pretend trip to look at churches in other parts of the world. They will follow you in an action at each location.

Tell the Story:

We are taking a pretend tour! We are going to visit Christian churches in other parts of the world. Buckle your seat belts. Here we go!

Our first stop is Brazil. Here the worshipers greet one another by shaking hands and saying, "Paz de Christo," which means "Peace of Christ." Let's all shake hands with one another and *say: "Paz de Christo."* (All shake hands and repeat words.)

Excellent! Buckle your seat belts again. We are off to Spain. Here in the huge cathedral, the girls cover their heads with lovely lace headscarves. Girls, let's put on our headscarves, which are called "mantillas." (Pretend to put on headscarves.) The cathedral is so big that you can hear echoes. Let's all *call out: Hello to the cathedral,* and listen for the echo. (*Call out and cup hands to ear, repeating: Hello to the cathedral in a softer voice. Repeat several times.*)

Buckle up again! We are in Denmark. Since the ship is a symbol for the church, some Danish churches have models of ships hanging from the ceilings. Let's look up and *say: There it is! The sailing ship.* (Look up, point, and repeat the words.)

Buckle up. We are in Ethiopia. In the city of Lalibela there are some very old churches built into volcanic rock. Let's go down a long slope and through a tunnel to get into one of these old churches. (Walk in place and then duck low and walk a bit more.) Here we are! Look at the interesting drawings on the walls. And I hear drummers. Let's make the sounds of drums with our hands. (Tap fist onto open palm.)

Buckle up one last time. Look at this wonderful church! (Describe your own church.) We are home! This is our church. Let's all *shout out: Hooray for (your church's name.)* (All shout hooray for your church.)

That was a great! I am glad we could visit Christian churches around the world!

Praying for Churches Around the World:

Say: Jesus told his disciples to "Go therefore and make disciples of all nations." This meant that they were to go to new places and tell others about him. Thanks to people who have carried the good news around the world, there are Christian churches everywhere! Because of the work of those disciples and many Christians since then, there are now Christian churches all over the world.

Have the children cross their arms to form a cross. Pray the Christian Church Prayer.

Exploring:

Children will create Ethiopian Art in honor of the wall paintings in Ethiopian churches. You will need paper, crayons, and tape.

Before Children's Church, tape the paper to the wall, one sheet per child. Make certain the paper is mounted at a height the children can easily reach.

Make a sample picture to show the children. Draw the design of an angel (triangle for a body, round head, triangle wings, and halo.) Draw crosses around the angel.

Ask: Do your parents let you write on the walls?

Say: Most of the time, parents don't want kids to draw on the walls; but today, we're going to pretend we are artists long ago in Ethiopia. We're going to decorate the walls of our church. Many of the artists drew or painted angels on the walls.

Show the children your angel picture. Point out that you added crosses to your picture and the children might want to add crosses, too.

Assign each child to a piece of paper. Comment on the drawings as the children work. When the drawings are finished, stand back and admire the Ethiopian Art.

Leave the art on the wall so the children can admire it in the weeks to come.

Snacking in Honor of Danish Boats:

In honor of the boats that decorate some churches in Denmark, serve the children Pear Boats. You will need pear halves, and raisins and/or marshmallows.

Say: In Denmark some churches have models of boats, which is a symbol of the church.

Give each child a pear slice.

Say: These pear halves are pretend boats. Now let's add some people to the boats.

Serve each child raisins and/or marshmallows to add to their boats.

Exploring Some More:

Play the echo game. Explain to the children that you are going to pretend to be in a Spanish cathedral listening for the echo. You will call out a phrase and they are to echo back to you. Cup your hand to your ear as you wait for the echo.

> **Hello Christians everywhere!** (children echo back)
> **Hello Churches of the World!** (children echo back)
> **Hooray for our church!** (children echo back)
> **Hooray for churches everywhere!** (children echo back)
> **Greetings to our brothers and sisters!** (children echo back)
> **May God bless all of us!** (children echo back)

Encourage the children to make up other phrases to be echoed.

Saying Goodbye:

Say: We can share God's love by learning about churches in faraway places and telling others what we have learned. We are glad there are Christian churches.

> Invite the children to echo after you:
> *It was fun to see you in Children's Church!*
> *Goodbye, Christians of the World!*

Christian Church Prayer:

God of Love, we are glad that there are Christian churches all over the world. Please take care of those churches and the people who worship there. Amen.

Supplies:

(for Exploring)
paper
crayons
tape

Snack:

pear halves
raisins and/or marshmallows
small bowls
spoons

Bible Verse:

"Now Joseph was taken down to Egypt." (Genesis 39:1)

OTHER LANDS

Opening a Newspaper:

Use a newspaper photo to introduce today's message. Find a picture that was taken in another country. Plan to give the children a brief explanation of the photo.

Gather the children together. Hold up the newspaper.

Say: Let's open the newspaper to see if we can find a photo taken in another land.

Show children the photo, and offer a simple explanation.

Say: Today we will learn about other lands from newspapers, television, the Internet, and from stories told by people who travel there. In Bible times, people learned about other lands from stories. Today, we're going to hear the story of a man from the Bible who visited another land.

Sharing a Story:

Use a toy animal to tell today's story. When the animal, named Jackie, in the story, turns a somersault, you will lead the children in *saying: And then what happened Jackie?* Use a silly voice for Jackie, and move the animal about as you speak.

Say: I have a friend named Jackie with me today. (Hold up the animal and have her say "Hello.") Today, Jackie wants to tell the story of Joseph. Joseph traveled to another land, the great land of Egypt. In the story, when Jackie turns a somersault, I want everyone to *ask in a loud voice: And then what happened Jackie?*

Practice this a few times, and then begin.

Tell the Story:

Once there lived a boy named Joseph. He had eleven brothers. His father, Jacob, loved Joseph very much. One day, he bought Joseph a fancy coat. (somersault)

All: And then what happened Jackie?

When his brothers saw the coat, they were very jealous and angry. (somersault)

All: And then what happened Jackie?

Joseph had a dream. When he told his brothers the dream, they got more angry. The dream made it seem like the brothers would bow down to Joseph. (somersault)

All: And then what happened Jackie?

The brothers decide to kill Joseph. (somersault)

All: And then what happened Jackie?

Reuben, a brother with a kind heart, said, "No." He told the other brothers to put Joseph in a pit. Reuben planned to rescue Joseph later. (somersault)

All: And then what happened Jackie?

They threw him in the pit. (somersault)

All: And then what happened Jackie?

A caravan with camels came by. They were on their way to Egypt. (somersault)

All: And then what happened Jackie?

The brothers sold Joseph to the caravan. (somersault)

All: And then what happened Jackie?

The travelers sold Joseph to a man who worked for the king of Egypt. (somersault)

All: And then what happened Jackie?

Joseph became important in Egypt. He explained dreams to the king. (somersault)

All: And then what happened Jackie?

Joseph became governor. (somersault)

All: And then what happened Jackie?

In time, his brothers went to Egypt because they needed food. (somersault)

All: And then what happened Jackie?

Joseph forgave them. And his whole family went to Egypt to live. The End.

Praying About Other Lands:

Say: When we learn about other lands, it helps us to understand the people who live there. When we understand people, we can better show them our love and concern.

Say: Let's make a circle and pray the Circle Prayer.

Exploring:

Children will make Egyptian Armlets. Many armlets were gold and embellished with jewels, so you might want to provide jewel stickers or round label stickers. Stickers can be found where office supplies are sold or in craft stores.

Before Children's Church, cut each sheet of paper in half vertically. You will be able to make two armlets from each sheet. If you want to make armlets for bigger kids or adults, you might need to tape on a bit more paper.

You may want to look for books on Egypt, art books, or encyclopedias for photos or drawings of armlets. Also look at Internet sites on ancient Egyptian jewelry and art.

Make a sample armlet to show the children.

Say: When Joseph arrived in Egypt, he may have seen men and women wearing fancy armlets. Today let's celebrate the land of Egypt by making our own armlets.

Ask a child to step forward. Use the sample to show how the armlet fits around the upper part of the arm. Show any photos or drawings, then invite the children to create their own armlets. As the children finish, tape or staple the armlet around their arm.

Snacking With an Egyptian Snack:

As you serve the snack, explain to the children that bakers used sesame seeds in ancient Egypt. Joseph might have enjoyed a similar snack.

Exploring Some More:

Play "Smile, You're in the Nile!"

Use the yarn to make a long oval-shaped stretch of pretend river.

Say: When Joseph was in Egypt, he saw the Nile River, the longest river in the world. Crocodiles live on some of the banks of the Nile. Let's pretend this yarn marks the Nile. When I call your name, jump into the Nile. Once everyone is in the Nile, I'll call you, one at a time, to jump out again.

Send the children into the Nile **saying: (Name), Jump! Jump! Jump into the Nile!** Call them out saying: Oh no! A crocodile! (Name), jump back out of the Nile!

If time permits, let other children take turns calling the group into and out of the Nile.

Saying Goodbye:

Ask the children to touch their armlet.

Say: One of the ways we share God's love is by learning about other lands and the people who live there. Goodbye, Learners of the World!

Circle Prayer:

God of Love, thank you for giving us a world filled with many lands and many people. Help us to learn all we can about other people and places. Amen.

Supplies:

(for Exploring)

copy paper
tape or stapler
crayons

gold seals or stars, jewel stickers, or round label stickers

picture(s) of Egyptian armlets

Snack:

crackers, bread, or breadsticks topped with sesame seeds

Supplies:

(for Exploring Some More)

a ball of yarn

**Bible
Verse:**

"Do not neglect
to do good and
to share what
you have."
(Hebrews 13:16)

Supplies:
(Opening a
Newspaper)

newspaper

Supplies:
(for Sharing
a Story)

a penny

a nickel

a dime

a quarter

a dollar bill

a twenty dollar bill

box or basket

SHARING CHRISTIANS

Opening a Newspaper:

Use photos of food and/or clothing in the newspaper to introduce today's message. Show these to the children.

Gather the children together. Hold up the newspaper.

Say: Inside this newspaper are photos of something that all people need.

Show children the photos.

Ask: What's this? (*food, clothing*) Why do people need this? (*We need it to live.*)

Say: There are people who do not have enough food or clothing. God wants us to share with these people. We can donate food and clothing to those who need it.

Sharing a Story:

Children will each take a turn holding the money. Place the money in a box or basket. Watch young children to make certain they do not put coins in their mouths.

Tell the Story:

Jingle the box or basket of money.

Ask: What do you think I just jingled? (*money*)

Say: As Christians, one of the ways we share God's love is with gifts of money.

Hold up a penny.

Ask: What's this? (*a penny*)

Say: When it's your time to hold the penny, *say: It's good to share our pennies.* (As the children pass the money, repeat the words along with them.)

Have the last child put the penny back in the box or basket. Hold up a nickel.

Ask: What's this? (*a nickel*)

Say: When it's your turn to hold the nickel, *say: It's good to share our nickels.*

Have the last child put the nickel back in the box or basket. Hold up the dime.

Ask: What's this? (*a dime*)

Say: When it's your turn to hold the dime, *say: It's good to share our dimes.*

Have the last child put the dime back into the box or basket. Hold up the quarter.

Ask: What's this? (*a quarter*)

Say: When it's your turn to hold the quarter, *say: It's good to share our quarters.*

Have the last child put the quarter back into the box or basket. Hold up the dollar bill.

Ask: What's this? (*a dollar bill*)

Say: When it's your turn to hold the dollar bill, *say: It's good to share our dollars.*

Have the last child put the dollar bill back into the box. Hold up the twenty dollar bill.

Ask: What's this? (*a twenty dollar bill*)

Say: When it's your turn to hold the twenty dollar bill, *say: It's good to share our twenty dollar bills.*

Have the last child put the twenty dollar bill back in the box or basket.

Say: A verse in the Bible talks about sharing. It is: "Do not neglect to do good and to share what you have" (Hebrews 13:16). I'm going to pass around the money in this box/basket. When it's your turn, jingle the money as you say the Bible verse.

100

Say the verse with the children. Take the box or basket back from the last child.

Say: The money we donate can be used to buy food and clothing that people around the world need. Thanks for helping me talk about sharing our money with others.

If your church supports a mission in this country or overseas, explain it to the children. Your pastor or a member of the mission committee may be able to provide a pamphlet to help the children see the work that is being done.

Praying About Money:

Have the children each put a hand or a finger on the box or basket of money. Ask them to close their eyes, then pray the Money Prayer.

Exploring:

Make a Share Your Coins Cups. Stickers are available where office supplies are sold.

Before Children's Church, enlarge the slit in each cup lid so that a coin can pass through. Make a sample Share Your Coins Cup to show the children. Use the round label stickers to create a cross on the outside of the cup.

Show the children the cup.

Say: This is a Share Your Coins Cup. You will make one, too. You can use your cup to collect coins for people who need our help.

Explain to the children that they will decorate their cups with a cross. This Christian symbol reminds us that God wants us to share our love with others. If your church collects coins for a specific mission, the coins collected can be designated for that cause. If your church does not collect coins for a specific mission, the children can put the coins they collect into the church offering.

When parents come to pick up their children, explain the project. Encourage parents to make donations to the Share Your Coins Cup, too.

Follow up with reminders in several weeks, so the children remember to bring the coins they have collected to church.

Snacking With a Cookie Coin:

Create cookie coins by wrapping round cookies in aluminum foil. Invite the children to admire their cookie coin before unwrapping and eating the cookie.

Exploring Some More:

Children will enjoy the challenge of a Coin Toss. Set out a large bowl, basket, or box. Have the children form a circle around it. Give each child five coins. (Use caution in allowing very young children to have coins.)

Invite the children to toss their coins into the container. As they toss each coin, ask them to *call out: Share what you have!*

If time permits, retrieve and distribute the coins and play again.

When the game is over, let the children put the coins into the Share Your Coins Cup.

Saying Goodbye:

Have the children hold their Share Your Coins Cup in the air. Ask them to *say after you: We will collect lots of coins! God wants us to share with people around the world!*

Say: When we share our money, we are sharing God's love by helping those who are in need. Goodbye, Sharers!

Money Prayer:
God of Love, help us to share our pennies and nickels and dimes and quarters and dollar bills with people around the world. Amen.

Supplies:
(for Exploring)

disposable hot/cold cups with lids

round label stickers

Snack:
round cookies

aluminum foil

Supplies:
(for Exploring Some More)

large bowl, basket, or box

five coins for each child

101

PRAYING FOR THE WORLD'S PEOPLE

Opening a Newspaper:

Use a photo from a newspaper to introduce today's message. Look through the paper to find one or several photos of people in another country who are in need of prayers.

Gather the children together. Hold up the newspaper.

Say: In this newspaper is a picture(s) of a person/people in another country who need our prayers.

Show children the photo(s.) Explain why the person/people need prayers. **For example: This man's home was washed away in a flood; or These children live in a country where a war is being fought.**

Say: Our prayers are one of the best ways to share God's love with people who live faraway.

Sharing a Story:

Today's story is a responsive prayer. Children will learn the Bible verse, then use the words of the verse as their response.

Say: Today, we are going to pray for God's people around the world. We will use this Bible verse from the Book of Psalms: "May the LORD give strength to his people!" (Psalm 29:11).

Have the children repeat the verse after you.

Ask: What does it mean for the Lord to give us strength? (*God will help us be brave. God will make us strong even when we have troubles. God will help us figure out how to make things better.*)

Say: When people have problems, God can help them have the courage, energy, and knowledge to work to make things better.

Lead the children in saying the verse. Then teach them these actions.

May the Lord: Arms high in the air, spread apart.

Give strength: Musicleman arms—arms bent at elbows, hands in fists facing upward.

To his people!: Use arms to gesture outward in a sweeping motion.

Explain to the children that you will end each line of the prayer with: Lord we pray. Then you will lead them in the response.

Tell the Story:

Let Us Pray:

For people who do not have nutritious food to eat, Lord we pray...

All: May the Lord give strength to his people! (add motions each time)

For people who do not have clean water to drink, Lord, we pray...

All: May the Lord give strength to his people!

For people who live where there are wars, Lord, we pray...

All: May the Lord give strength to his people!

For children who do not have any parents, Lord, we pray...

102

All: May the Lord give strength to his people!

For people who have lost their homes because of floods and earthquakes,
Lord, we pray...

All: May the Lord give strength to his people!

For people who cannot visit doctors and hospitals when they are sick, Lord,
we pray...

All: May the Lord give strength to his people!

For people who are sad, lonely, worried, and angry; Lord, we pray...

All: May the Lord give strength to his people!

Amen.

Praying for Children Around the World:

Lead children in an action prayer that honors children around the world.

Say: Kids love to play. All over the world, kids play every day. Let's celebrate
with a prayer. Follow my actions. Pray the Action Prayer.

Exploring:

To make Prayer Pennants you will need felt, scissors, and glue. Purchase felt squares,
one square for every two children. You also need additional felt to cut decorative pieces.

Before Children's Church, cut two pennants from each felt square. Next, you will
need to cut a felt circle that will fit inside the widest part of the pennant and a heart
that will fit inside the circle for each pennant. Tacky craft glue is best for gluing felt.
Make a sample pennant to show the children.

Say: Let's make Prayer Pennants! (Wave the sample pennant.) **The circle represents
our world. The heart reminds us to pray for the people of God's world.**

Give each child a pennant. Invite them to wave their pennants, *saying: We pray for
the people of God's world!*

Then have the children glue on the felt world. Next have them glue the heart on top
of the world.

Say: Now you have a Prayer Pennant to keep in your room at home. Remember
that one way you can share God's love with the world is through your prayers.
When you look at your Prayer Pennant, it will remind you to pray for the people
of the world.

Snacking With Bread:

Serve children one or more types of international bread such as flatbread, Italian or
French bread, rye bread, focaccia, or raisin bread. Cut the bread into small pieces.

Say: People throughout the world eat bread. It is fun to try breads from other lands!

As you serve the snack, explain to the children what type of bread they will be eating.

As children enjoy their bread, ask them what type of bread they eat at their house.

Ask: Do you like to make sandwiches with a certain kind of bread? Do you toast
your bread? Do you like it with butter, jam, honey, cream cheese, or another spread?

Action Prayer:

God of Love,
bless the kids
who build castles
on the beaches
of Australia.
(Pretend to dig
and pat sand.)

Bless the kids
who splash on the
shores of
South Africa.
(Pretend to
splash water.)

Bless the kids
who slide on the
ice in Russia.
(Pretend to slide.)

Bless the kids
who swing from
vines in Brazil.
(Pretend to hold
onto a vine.)

Bless the kids
who fly kites
in Japan.
(Pretend to fly
a kite.)

And bless us, too.
(Place hands
across chest.)

Amen.

Supplies:

(for Exploring)

felt squares

sharp scissors
(for teacher's use)

glue (tacky craft
type, if possible)

Snack:

international
breads

Supplies:

(for Exploring
Some More)

posterboard or
a large sheet of
craft paper

newspapers
and/or magazines

scissors

glue

a marker
or crayon

Exploring Some More:

Make a World's People Prayer Poster.

Children will glue photos onto the poster. Before Children's Church, cut photos of people from newspapers and magazines. (If you have older children, they may be able to search the newspapers and magazines to find the pictures themselves.) At the top of the poster write: "Remember To Pray For the World's People."

Bring out the poster. Read the heading to the children.

Next, invite the children to create a World's People Prayer Poster. They may glue on the pictures however they choose, but if you have a good number of pictures, encourage the children to glue them close to one another. When the poster is finished, hold it up for all to appreciate.

Say: We will hang our World's People Prayer Poster in our church. When the people in our congregation see the poster, they will be reminded to pray for the people of the world.

Hang the poster somewhere in the church where everyone can see it.

Saying Goodbye:

Have children wave their Prayer Pennants.

Say: We share God's love when we pray for the people of the world. Goodbye, Children of Prayer!

104

LIGHT OF THE WORLD

Opening a Newspaper:

Introduce the message by showing the children a candle hidden in a newspaper. Either cut out a large paper candle and tape it to a page of the newspaper, or color a candle onto a page.

Gather the children together. Hold up the newspaper.

Say: Let's see what is hidden in this newspaper.

Open the newspaper and begin to turn the pages until you come to the candle.

Say: My something is shining on me! Something is making a lot of light!

Ask: What is this? (*a candle*)

Say: Candles make light! As Christians, we are called to be lights of the world.

Sharing a Story:

Children will use their pointer fingers as pretend candles. They will make this gesture and *say: Live as children of light* when you give them the cue. Use the candle gesture yourself to cue them each time.

Say: In the Bible, Paul tells Christians to "live as children of light." This means that we are to live the way God wants us to live. In today's story, we will talk about ways to live as children of light. But first let's make pretend candles.

Show the children how to hold up their pointer finger to represent a candle.

Say: When I hold up my candle, hold up yours too, and *say along with me: Live as children of light.*

Practice this a few times, and then begin.

Tell the Story:

There was a terrible tidal wave that destroyed many homes. Becky and Ben sold lemonade all summer to raise money for the people who lost their homes. In the fall, they put the money in a special offering their church was collecting. The offering helped the people build new homes. (candle gesture)

All: Live as children of light.

Holly's church was collecting cans for the local food bank. The food bank gives food to people who are hungry. Holly used her allowance to buy ten cans of chicken noodle soup. She brought the soup to church and put it in the collection box. (candle gesture)

All: Live as children of light.

Maura has a cousin who is serving in the Peace Corps. Her cousin is starting a school for children in a remote village in Africa. Maura wrote her cousin a letter and included stickers for her to share with all the children there. (candle gesture)

All: Live as children of light.

A new girl came to Liza's class. She did not speak any English. Liza smiled at her during spelling and math. At lunchtime, she motioned for the new girl to sit next to her in the cafeteria. (candle gesture)

All: Live as children of light.

Seth's dad is serving in the army. When he came home on leave, he told Seth about a little boy he met who did not have many toys. Seth sent two of his new toys back with his dad. His dad will give them to the boy. (candle gesture)

Message:
Christians are called to be lights to the world.

Verse:
"Live as children of light." (Ephesians 5:8)

Supplies:
(Opening a Newspaper)

newspaper

paper

scissors

tape

crayon

Prayer:

God of Love,
(children repeat)

help us,
(children repeat)

day and night,
(children repeat)

to walk
as children,
(children repeat)

of your light.
(children repeat)

Amen.
(children repeat)

Supplies:
(for Exploring)

small, clear
plastic plates
(1 per child)

yellow tissue
paper

scissors

paint pen or bold
permanent marker

glue

tape

yarn

All: Live as children of light.

Last night on the news, Brittany heard of a terrible fire in a town not too far from hers. Several firefighters were injured. At dinner, she offered a prayer for the firefighters. (candle gesture)

All: Live as children of light.

Kim's mother is a doctor. She is going to another country for two weeks to help take care of sick children there. Kim asked her class to bring in donations of adhesive bandages for her mother to take with her. They collected seventy-eight boxes. (candle gesture)

All: Live as children of light.

The pastor at Shamika's church is going on a trip to a country where there was an earthquake. He will be helping rebuild a church there. Shamika's Sunday school class made cards for their pastor to give to the children at that church. (candle gesture)

All: Live as children of light.

On starry nights, Ellie likes to look up at the stars and say this prayer, "Dear God, please take care of all the people in the world who are hungry and cold and sad. Amen." (candle gesture)

All: Live as children of light.

Praying About Light:

Ask the children to hold up their pretend candles again. Have them repeat each line of the prayer after you.

Exploring:

Children will make Child of Light Circles to hang in a window at home. Before Children's Church, use a permanent marker to print: "Child of light" on the inside of each plate. Cut or tear the tissue paper into pieces about two or three inches wide.

Make a sample Child of Light Circle. Glue the tissue paper to the back side of the plate, overlapping the tissue as you work. Use tape to attach a twelve-inch length of yarn to the top of the plate. Tape the yarn in the middle of the length, leaving the ends free for tying.

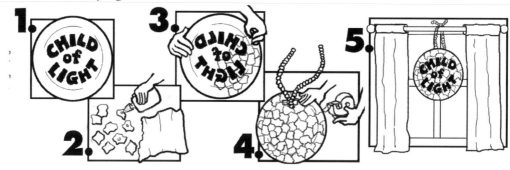

Say: God wants us to live as children of light. We're going to make Child of Light Circles to hang in a window at home.

Show the children the sample. Explain that on sunny days, the light will shine through the tissue paper. On darker days, the yellow tissue will remind them of sunny light.

When the children are finished, help each child attach a length of yarn to their Child of Light Circles. Explain that at home, they can ask a grownup to help them tie the yarn around a curtain rod or another part of the window.

Snacking:

In honor of light, serve a yellow snack such as lemon or vanilla pudding, lemon yogurt, or lemon sherbet.

As children enjoy their snacks, ask them to share any adventures they have had with darkness such as taking a nighttime walk with their grandpa, or the week the power went out because of the hurricane. Say a thank-you prayer before eating.

Exploring Some More:

Lead children in singing "This Little Light of Mine:"

> **Sing:** This little light of mine, I'm going to let it shine,
>
> This little light of mine, I'm going to let it shine,
>
> This little light of mine, I'm going to let it shine,
>
> Let it shine, let it shine, let it shine.

Words: African-American spiritual (Matthew 5:14-16)

Once children know the verse, have them hold their pointer fingers in the air to represent a candle. Sing the verse a few more times as the children move their pretend candles back and forth.

Next, teach them a new verse to the song:

> **Sing:** Live as children of light, show God's love to the world,
>
> Live as children light, show God's love to the world,
>
> Live as children of light, show God's love to the world,
>
> Show God's love, show God's love, show God's love.

Words: Lisa Flinn and Barbara Younger; © 2007 Abingdon Press.

After the children know this verse, show them how to put one hand on each side of their face, with fingers spread apart, to imitate rays of light. Sing this verse a few more times as children turn their heads from side to side with their hands in this position.

Saying Goodbye:

Ask the children to put their hands up to their faces again.

Say: You are beautiful children of light. Go and share God's love with the world. Goodbye, Children of Light!

Send the Child of Light Circles home with the children.

Supplies:

(Opening a
Newspaper)

photo in a
newspaper of
someone working
for peace

PEACE POLES

Opening a Newspaper:

Use a newspaper photo to introduce today's message. Look through the paper to find a photo of someone working for peace. (A relief worker, a soup kitchen volunteer, a nurse, a teacher, a member of the clergy, college students doing volunteer work.) If you cannot find a photograph in the paper, locate one in a news magazine or from the Internet, then put the photo inside the newspaper.

Gather the children together. Hold up the newspaper.

Ask: What is peace. (*When people get along. When people do not fight. When people are good to one another.*)

Say: Let's see if we can find a peace picture in this newspaper. We are going to look for someone who is helping make the world a better, more peaceful place.

Turn the pages of the newspaper until you get to the photo. Explain to the children how the person in the photo is working for peace.

Say: God wants us to show our love to the world by working for peace. Listen to this Bible verse from Psalm 34: "Seek peace and pursue it." That means to look for peace and to work to make the world a peaceful place.

Have the children say the verse after you.

Sharing a Story:

The children will hear about the Peace Pole Project. (They will create a peace pole for the church to sign.) There are many references on the Internet to the idea of a Peace Pole. You might want to check out this website: http://www.worldpeace.org/peace-poles.html, or some of the other sites. Consider printing out some photos of Peace Poles for the children to see.

Tell the Story:

There are people all over the world who work for peace. They believe that we can best share God's love by being kind and loving to one another. Some of these people build Peace Poles.

A Peace Pole is usually a long piece of wood. The words: May Peace Prevail on Earth are written on the pole. People who make peace poles know that praying to God for peace can help bring peace to our world. The pole is usually very tall, taller than a grownup. One end of it is planted into the ground so that it will stand straight.

Peace Poles have been planted all over the world. There are Peace Poles at churches like ours and there are Peace Poles in famous places like the pyramids in Egypt and the Magnetic North Pole in Canada. Many towns and cities have peace poles.

When the Peace Pole is in place, the people who have planted it usually hold a ceremony. Everyone gathers around the pole. They sing songs and say prayers, asking for peace in our world.

Today, we are going to decorate and sign our very own Peace Pole!

Praying About Peace:

Have the children form a close circle. Ask them to stack their hands on one another's hands, to form a pretend Peace Pole. (If your group is large you may have to create several pretend poles.) Pray the Peace Prayer.

Peace
Prayer:
God of Love,
may peace
prevail on
earth!
Help us
to seek peace
in all we do.
Amen.

Exploring:

Children will decorate and sign a Peace Pole.

If you have someone in your congregation who is willing to take on the task of creating a Peace Pole out of wood, refer that person to the website listed earlier. If not, make a simple Peace Pole using hard foam board. Purchase a sheet of foam board in any color. Cut the board into thirds, lengthwise. Tape the lengths together to form a tall Peace Pole.

The Peace Pole will later be presented to the congregation. Everyone will be invited to sign their names on the pole. You might want to present the pole during a children's sermon or at a church fellowship event. If you have a Peace Pole made of wood, plan on planting it at your church. If you have a Peace Pole made from hard foam board, you can display it inside the church for all to see.

Use a marker to write: "May Peace Prevail on Earth" down the length of a pole.

Say: This is our Peace Pole. It says: May Peace Prevail on Earth.

Ask: What are some of the ways we can work for peace? (*Do not fight. Be kind to others. Help people who have problems. Work to prevent or stop war.*)

Say: Let's all sign our names to the Peace Pole!

After the children sign their names, invite them to draw a flower, butterfly, cross, or heart next to their name, as a symbol of peace.

Explain to your children when the congregation will sign the Peace Pole and where it will be placed after all have signed.

Snacking With a Pretzel Pole:

In honor of Peace Poles, serve the children pretzel rods.

Say: We're having Pretzel Poles today in honor of our Peace Pole.

As the children enjoy their snacks, invite them to share personal stories of peace-making such as the time they encouraged their little sisters to stop fighting or the time they refused to argue with their big brother when he was teasing them. Say a prayer for peace before eating the snack.

Exploring Some More:

Children will enjoy making Personal Peace Poles to keep at home.

Give each child a craft stick.

Say: We decorated a beautiful, tall Peace Pole today to keep at church. Now, let's make Personal Peace Poles to keep at home.

Children who can write, can copy the word "Peace" from the large Peace Pole. You can write "Peace" for younger children.

Next, encourage the children to decorate their tiny Peace Poles with fanciful designs such as dots and squiggles.

Say: When you get home, tuck your Peace Pole into your pencil cup, a plant, or some other place where you will see it every day!

Saying Goodbye:

Have the children each touch the Peace Pole.

Say: Remember to pray for peace and work for peace every day! Goodbye, Peacemakers!

If you have made Personal Peace Poles, be sure to send them home with the children.

Sharing God's Love in Our World

Supplies:

(for Exploring)

hard foam board and bold, permanent markers
sturdy tape
cutting tool

Snack:

pretzel rods

Supplies:

(for Exploring Some More)

craft sticks
(1 per child)

markers

Chapter 7

Sharing God's Love
DURING HOLIDAYS

THE NEW YEAR:
Count Your Blessings

Message:

We count our blessings as the New Year begins.

Verse:

"You crown the year with your bounty." (Psalm 65:11)

Supplies:

(for Opening a Gift Box)

box with lid

festive wrapping paper and bow

tape

calendar for the new year

Supplies:

(for Sharing a Story)

toy animal

Opening a Gift Box:

Cover a box and a lid with festive wrapping paper. Add a bow to the lid. To introduce the message, put a calendar for the new year in the box.

Gather the children together. Hold up the gift box. Choose a child to open the box and pull out what's inside.

Ask: What's this? (*a calendar*)

Say: This is a calendar for the brand new year.

Ask: What is the name of the new year?

Say: Let's all say that together. (*Everyone says the year.*) Let's say it one more time in our most enthusiastic voices. (*Everyone says the year again.*)

Turn the pages of the calendar. Point out a few important days such as Valentine's Day, Easter, Christmas, and your own birthday.

Say: Look at all those days! We are glad God has given us one more year filled with lots of days. The brand new year is one of God's many blessings.

Sharing a Story:

In today's story an animal, named Sport, will talk to the children about his many blessings. After each line of the story, Sport will pause while the children count the blessings just named. Find a toy animal to play the role of Sport. Use a silly voice for Sport and move the animal about as it speaks.

Tell the Story:

(If children have trouble coming up with the correct number of blessings, say the line of the story again. Hold up a finger as each blessing is added.)

Hi! My name is Sport. Happy New Year, Everybody! I am really excited that God has given me a brand new year. I love the thought of all those days to come.

God has blessed me in so many ways. When an old year ends and a new year begins, that is an especially good time for me to count my blessings. Will you help me?

I have one nice home where I live. How many blessings is that? (*one*)

Two grownups take care of me. My mom and my grandma. How many blessings is that? (*two*)

110

I have a sister named Jump and a sister named Skip, and a sister named Dance. How many blessings is that? (*three*)

I have a brother named Hop, and a brother named Run, and a brother named Tag, and a brother named Leap. How many blessings is that? (*four*)

I have a friend named Sing, and a friend named Paint, and a friend named Swim, and a friend named Sleep, and a friend named Cook. How many blessings is that? (*five*)

I go to a really nice church. How many blessings is that? (*one*)

I like the big stained-glass window in the back and the cross in the front. How many blessings is that? (*two*)

I sing in the choir; I love to hear the organ; and our pastor is nice. How many blessings is that? (*three*)

At Children's Church I like the stories, and the crafts, and the prayers, and the games. How many blessings is that? (*four*)

At church suppers I always eat macaroni and brownies and fruit and biscuits and string beans. How many blessings is that? (*five*)

I can do a great cartwheel. How many blessings is that? (*one*)

I like to read and color. How many blessings is that? (*two*)

I have a jump rope and a fuzzy blanket and a cup with my name on it. How many blessings is that? (*three*)

I get to go to school, to the pool, to the park, and to the sub shop. How many blessings is that? (*four*)

My home is warm, my bed is soft, my food tastes good, my clothes are clean, and my family loves me. How many blessings is that? (*five*)

Thanks, everybody, for helping me to count my blessings. As the old year ends and a new one begins, you should count your blessings, too!

Praying About Blessings:

Say: There is a verse in the Bible that says, "You crown the year with your bounty" (Psalm 65:11). That means that God gives us blessings every year.

Ask the children to say the Bible verse along with you.

Next, explain that when you begin to count during the prayer, they are to join in. You will count to ten, just for fun, even though everyone has lots more than ten blessings. Pray the Blessings Prayer.

Exploring:

Children will make Welcome New Year Magnets. Glitter and adhesive magnetic strips can be found in craft departments and stores. You might want to use food storage bags for sending the magnets home.

Before Children's Church, cut magnetic strips to fit on the back of the index cards. You can attach the strips to the cards ahead of time, or do it with the children.

Say: We are going to make Welcome New Year Magnets. You can keep the magnet on your refrigerator at home to welcome the new year and to remember to count your blessings.

If you have not attached the magnetic strips ahead of time, have the children do so now.

Next, ask them to turn the card so the blank side is facing up. Go from child to child and write the numbers of the new year with a thick line of glue. (Older children may be able to do this themselves.) Then, have the child place the card in the pan and

Blessings Prayer:

God of Love, thank you for the old year (number of year), and the brand new year (number of year). Help us to remember to count our blessings: One, two, three (count to ten). Counting our blessings helps us understand how good you have been to us.

Amen.

Supplies:

(for Exploring)

index cards

glue

glitter

adhesive magnetic strips

a pan

food storage bags

111

shake glitter to cover the numbers. Once the glitter has completely covered the numbers, have the child gently shake the remaining glitter off the card.

When it is time to send the magnets home, consider placing each child's Welcome New Year Magnet in a food storage bag.

Snack:

mini-marshmallows colored candies, raisins, or chocolate chips

cake,
pan of brownies,
bowl of gelatin,
or another snack

Supplies:

(for Exploring Some More)

calendar for the new year

Snacking for the New Year:

Use mini-marshmallows, colored candies, raisins, or chocolate chips to decorate a cake, pan of brownies, bowl of gelatin, or another snack with the numbers of the new year.

Say: Hooray for the new year, (number of year), and the many blessings we enjoy!

Exploring Some More:

Use a calendar for the new year to point out some more important days to come. After each day is pointed out, let the children say what they like best about that day.

Saying Goodbye:

Have the children look at their Welcome New Year Magnets.

Say: We are glad that God crowns the year with bounty and gives us so many blessings. Counting our blessings and sharing our blessings with others is a great way to celebrate God's love in the new year. Happy New Year! Goodbye, Blessing Counters!

EPIPHANY:
Saying "Thank You"

Opening a Gift Box:

Cover a box and a lid with festive wrapping paper. Add a bow to the lid. To introduce the message, wrap up today's snack, or part of the snack, in wrapping paper and ribbon. Put the package in the box.

Gather the children together. Hold up the gift box.

Say: I wonder what our present is today.

Call a child forward to open the box and take out the package.

Say: Why it looks like another present!

Thank the child and call another child forward to unwrap the present.

Say: Our snack! We'll enjoy this present in a little while, when it's snack time.

Ask: Can you each tell me a present you received for Christmas?

Say: Receiving presents is lots of fun. Do you know what else is fun and important? Saying, "Thank you!"

Sharing a Story:

Today's story of the wise men (Matthew 2:1-12) is told in rhyme. When the children hear a long pause, they are to fill in the missing rhyme. If children have trouble figuring out the rhyming answer, say it for them. Consider using pictures or figures of the wise men to tell the story.

Tell the Story:

This is the story of the wise men who gave presents to baby Jesus. When I pause, fill in the missing rhyme. Ready?

We are wise men, travelers from afar, off to find Jesus by following a _____ (*star.*)

Look at the star! How bright and fine! My how that beautiful star does_____ (*shine.*)

For the baby they say is born to be king, three kinds of presents we will _____ (*bring.*)

One gift we want the baby to behold, is a precious metal, a gift of _____ (*gold.*)

On this journey we've set out to make, frankincense is a gift we'll _____ (*take.*)

Myrrh's a good gift, a special perfume, I hope we find the baby ____ (*soon.*)

The star's up ahead, off we go! Let's hurry up. Let's not be ____ (*slow.*)

Finally we're here, we feel such joy. We bow down and worship the baby ____ (*boy.*)

We give him our presents. "Thank you," says the mother, "from baby and _____ " (*me.*)

Say: The Bible doesn't actually tell us that Mary said "thank you" for the presents. Do you think she did?

Mary probably did say "thank you" for the lovely gifts. Gold was a valuable metal. Frankincense and myrrh were valuable, too. They were used in perfumes.

If time permits, lead the children in filling in the rhyming words another time or two.

Praying About Gifts:

Say: One way to show God's love is by thanking people for their gifts. During the prayer, when I pause, picture in your mind a gift that someone gave you this Christmas.

Message:
We say "thank you" for gifts.

Bible Verse:
"Then, opening their treasure chests, they offered him gifts of gold, frankincense, and myrrh." (Matthew 2:11)

Supplies:
(for Opening a Gift Box and Share a Story)

box with lid

festive wrapping paper and bow

ribbon and tape

today's snack

pictures or figures of the wise men (optional)

Prayer:
God of Love, we are glad that the wise men gave baby Jesus gifts. Right now, we will picture a Christmas present (pause). Please help us to remember to thank people for the gifts they give us. Amen.

113

Supplies:

(for Exploring)

old Christmas cards

blank note cards
or 4-by-6
index cards

glue

craft scissors

markers, crayons,
or a "Thank You"
stamp and ink pad

Exploring:

The children will trim old Christmas cards to decorate the front of note cards or index cards. Tear the front off the cards to make trimming the cards easier for the children.

Blank note cards can be found in stationery sections, craft sections, and many dollar stores. Or use blank index cards. They are less expensive and will make fine postcards. If possible, locate a "Thank You" stamp for the children to enjoy using. If not, those who know how to write, can write "Thank You" on their cards. Assist non-writers. Craft scissors that create unusual borders will add to the fun.

Ask: Can you each tell me the name of someone you would like to thank for a Christmas present?

Say: Let's make Christmas Thank-You Cards! You may give or send the card to the person you want to thank.

As the children watch, make a sample card to show them. Trim around a Christmas card so that the picture on the card will fit onto a blank card. Comment on why that Christmas card was chosen and what a nice thank-you card it will make.

Next invite the children to make one or several cards. Have them write or stamp "Thank You" onto the inside of the card (for note cards) and onto the blank, left-hand side of the index card (for postcards).

Tell the children that they should sign their name to their card/cards and give or send the card(s) as soon as possible.

Sharing a Snack Gift:

Bring out the snack, which was unwrapped earlier.

While the children enjoy the snack, ask them to talk about the presents they gave this holiday season, as well as the presents they received.

Exploring Some More:

Supplies:

(for Exploring
Some More)

several patterns
of holiday
gift-wrapping

posterboard

scissors

glue

construction paper

marker

Several patterns of wrapping paper will be needed for this activity. Cut the gift-wrapping into three- or four-inch squares or into rectangles. (This is a great use for leftover or recycled gift-wrapping.)

Say: Let's make a Giant Present Collage!

Invite the children to glue the gift-wrapping pieces onto the posterboard, putting the pieces as close together as possible.

Use the construction paper to create a bow, either flat or three-dimensional, to glue to the top of the Present Collage. Add a sign that says: Thanks to God for Jesus, Our Greatest Gift.

Say: Our beautiful Giant Present Collage thanks God for the gift of Jesus, the greatest Christmas present of all. Let's hang it up for the whole church to see!

As soon as possible, hang the Giant Present Collage in a good location.

Saying Goodbye:

Send the Christmas Thank-You Cards home with the children.

Say: Thanking people for the gifts they give us is a great way to share God's love. It is important to say "thank you!" Goodbye, Thankers!

VALENTINE'S DAY:
"L" Stands for "Love"

Introduce the Message:

Cover a box and a lid with festive wrapping paper. Add a bow to the lid.

During Exploring, children will decorate valentines. To introduce the message, use some of those craft materials to create a pretty paper heart with a large letter "L" in the center of the heart. Place the heart in the box.

Gather the children. Hold up the gift box. Ask a child to hold up what's inside.

Ask: What's this? (*a heart, a valentine*) What letter do you see on the heart? (*an "L"*) We're going to talk about Valentine's Day today, a day that celebrates love. Why do you think there's an "L" on this heart? (*Because "L" stands for "Love."*)

Say: "L" stands for Love. God loves us and wants us to show love to others.

Sharing a Story:

During the story, when the letter "L" is held up, the children will *call out: "L" stands for Love!* As they do, they will hold their arms above their heads, with their hands bent down together, to form the shape of a heart. Demonstrate this gesture for them.

Tell the Story:

The night before Valentine's Day, Meg remembered that she had forgotten to make her dad a valentine. She made him a really pretty one, with a big "L" on the front with glitter glue because…(hold up heart)

All: "L" stands for love.

When she went to breakfast, she gave everyone a big hug. She said, "I Love you." As she said it, she said the "L" with extra oomph because…(hold up heart)

All: "L" stands for love.

At school, Meg helped a boy who had dropped the cupcakes he was bringing. The boy was crying. They were able to rescue all of the cupcakes. She told him, "Don't be sad. Today is a really happy day. A Letter 'L' Day, because…" (hold up heart)

All: "L" stands for love.

On the playground, Meg and her friends made a big "L" in the sand. They called their teacher over. "Ms. Allen," Meg said. "This 'L' is for you, because…" (hold up heart)

All: "L" stands for love.

In the cafeteria, she gave the ladies behind the counter a note. It said, "Ladies, Thanks lots for the lovely lunches. Love, Meg." Meg used plenty of "L's" because… (hold up heart)

All: "L" stand for love.

After lunch, they had art. Their teacher had a cool, new paint. Meg decided she would mail her painting to her grandma who was sick. She made beautiful hearts and "L's" all over her painting because… (hold up heart)

All: "L" stands for love.

That afternoon, Meg helped her mom clean up for the Valentine's dinner they were having that night. She drew an "L" in the dust before she dusted the TV because… (hold up heart)

All: "L" stands for love.

Message:
We celebrate God's gift of love.

Bible Verse:
"Beloved, let us love one another, because love is from God." (1 John 4:7)

Supplies:
(for Opening a Gift Box)

box with lid

festive wrapping paper

bow

craft materials

heart with the letter "L" on it

Supplies:
(for Sharing a Story)

heart you made

Love Prayer:

God of Love, we thank you for your great gift of love. Help us to show love at all times. We're glad that "L" stands for love! Amen.

Supplies:

(for Exploring)

construction paper

glue

markers or crayons

Consider other craft materials such as: paper doilies, stickers, glitter glue tubes or pens

foam shapes

decorated papers such as wrapping paper, wallpaper, and scrap-booking paper

Snack:

choose a snack from choice 1 or 2

Supplies:

(for Exploring Some More)

same as for Exploring

At dinner, she said to her mom, "Thanks for the great food." Then she lined up the peas on her plate to make an "L" because...(hold up heart)

All: "L" stands for love.

When dinner was over, she helped load the dishwasher and scrub the pots and pans. There were plenty of soap bubbles. She used the bubbles to make the letter "L" on the kitchen counter because... (hold up heart)

All: "L" stands for love.

After dinner, she and her family played an alphabet game. Meg was a pretty good speller. When it was her turn, she said, "This is how I feel about all of you." Then she wrote the word: "L-O-V-E" because.... (hold up heart)

All: "L" stands for love.

When she got into bed that night, Meg prayed: "Dear God, help me to show love every day, not just on Valentine's Day. But thanks for such a fun Valentine's Day. This has been a Letter "L" day..." (hold up heart)

All: "L" stands for love.

Praying About Love:

Say: There's a verse in the Bible about Love. Listen to this lovely verse.

Say the verse, 1 John 4:7, for the children, then have them repeat it with you. Have them hold up their thumbs and index fingers to form the Letter "L." Pray the Love Prayer.

Exploring:

Before Children's Church, cut construction paper into large hearts. In contrasting colors of paper, cut large "L's." Use other colors and patterns to cut smaller hearts.

Say: "L" stands for lots of wonderful things in God's world such as lions, lakes, ladybugs, light, and lizards. But today, we are going to put the letter "L" on valentines in honor of love.

Suggest that the children first glue an "L" onto their heart, then decorate the rest of their valentines. Tell them they may give their valentines to someone they love.

Snacking With the Letter L:

Celebrate the Letter "L" with a snack. Here are two snack ideas:

1) Serve snacks that begin with the letter "L" such as lollipops; lady fingers (any oval-shaped cookies or cakes will do); lemonade; lemon- or lime-flavored cookies, cake, pudding, yogurt, or sherbet; licorice; or lemon drops.

2) Use frosting from a tube to drizzle the letter "L" on graham crackers or another type of cookie or cake.

Exploring Some More:

Have the children make more valentines. Explain that these valentines will be passed on to your pastor. The pastor visits people who are sick, lonely, and sad. These people will love to receive beautiful valentines made by the kids in Children's Church.

Saying Goodbye:

Have the children hold their Letter "L" Valentine.

Say: We're glad that "L" stands for love. Give your Letter "L" Valentine to someone you love. What a great way to share God's love with someone special. Goodbye, Loving Kids!

116

PALM SUNDAY:
Jesus Rode a Donkey

Opening a Gift Box:

Cover a box and a lid with festive wrapping paper. Add a bow to the lid. To introduce the message, put a donkey puppet into the box. (See Exploring for directions on how to make the puppet.)

Gather the children together. Hold up the gift box. Choose a child to take off the lid, lift the puppet out, and slip it on.

Say: This is Brady the Donkey! He's a puppet. I named him Brady since donkeys say "Braa-aaa–y." When Brady opens his mouth, we can help him say, "Braa-aaa-y."

Have the child make the puppet open its mouth several times as everyone *calls out: Braa-aaa-y.*

Put the puppet on your own hand.

Say: Today, Brady the donkey is going to help me tell the story of Palm Sunday. On Palm Sunday, Jesus rode a donkey into Jerusalem.

Sharing a Story:

Use the donkey puppet to tell the story of Jesus' ride into Jerusalem (John 12:12-14). The children will join in by *calling out: braaa-aaa-y* when Brady the Donkey opens his mouth wide. As the story is told, speak in a silly voice and make the puppet move about, but only open his mouth as a cue to the children.

Tell the Story:

Brady the Donkey is pleased to tell you the story of Palm Sunday. He wants you to help tell the story by *calling out: Braa-aaa-y* when he opens his mouth wide.

Hi, everybody! I want to tell you the story of a very exciting day. Every time I think about it, I want to bray really loud. (open puppet mouth)

Children: *Braa-aaa-y.*

I am a very young donkey. Let's hear it for young donkeys and kids! (open puppet mouth)

Children: *Braa-aaa-y.*

There was a big festival and people were everywhere. The people heard that Jesus was coming to Jerusalem. (open puppet mouth)

Children: *Braa-aaa-y.*

So they took branches of palm trees (open puppet mouth)

Children: *Braa-aaa-y.*

And they went out to meet him shouting, "Hosanna!" (open puppet mouth)

Children: *Braa-aaa-y.*

They shouted, "Blessed is the one who comes in the name of the Lord." (open mouth)

Children: *Braa-aaa-y.*

They called him the "King of Israel!" (open puppet mouth)

Children: *Braa-aaa-y.*

Then he came and found me! (open puppet mouth)

Children: *Braa-aaa-y.*

Bible Verse:
"Jesus found a young donkey and sat on it." (John 12:14)

Supplies:
(for Opening a Gift Box)
box with lid
festive wrapping paper
bow
donkey puppet

Supplies:
(for Sharing a Story)
donkey puppet

The only thing I could think of to say was... (open puppet mouth)

Children: *Braa-aaa-y.*

Jesus got on my back (open puppet mouth)

Children: *Braa-aaa-y.*

And he rode on me through the crowds of people. (open puppet mouth)

Children: *Braa-aaa-y.*

We rode through all the people waving palm branches (open puppet mouth)

Children: *Braa-aaa-y.*

And shouting, "Hosanna!" (open puppet mouth)

Children: *Braa-aaa-y.*

What a day that was, (open puppet mouth)

Children: *Braa-aaa-y.*

The day Jesus, the Savior, rode on me into Jerusalem, (open puppet mouth)

Children: *Braa-aaa-y.*

A day we call Palm Sunday. (open puppet mouth)

Children: *Braa-aaa-y.*

Thanks for listening to my story!

Praying About Palm Sunday:

Have the children hold up their hands with their fingers spread apart.

Say: Some say the palm tree got its name because its branches look like the palms of our hands. Let's hold up our palms to be palm branches during the prayer. Pray the Palm Sunday Prayer.

Exploring:

Make a donkey puppet to be used in the opening and for the story. During Exploring, each child will also make a puppet. The donkey's ears can be cut from brown construction paper, but using felt will make the ears soft, like a real donkey's ears.
(1) On the flap of the paper bag, use a crayon to draw the nose and eyes of a donkey.
(2) Next, open the flap and give the donkey a set of teeth and a tongue. (3) Cut large ears out of felt or construction paper. (4) Staple these to the top of the donkey's head.
(5) Cut four legs from brown construction paper, and staple these to the donkey's body, extending out from the edges of the paper bag, two on each side.

When it is time to make the puppet with the children, take them through each step. Then have the children put them on and practice making the puppets talk.

Say: Now we have a room full of Brady the Donkeys! Let's hear all of the Bradys say "Braaa-aaa-y" at the same time!

Explain that they can take their puppets home to tell others the story of Palm Sunday.

Snacking on Straw:

Serve each child a cracker or two, topped with grated cheese.

Say: Donkeys like to eat straw. We are going to pretend this cheese is straw, in honor of Brady and all of the donkeys of the world.

Exploring Some More:

Children will have fun acting out a Palm Sunday Parade.

Say: When Jesus rode a donkey into Jerusalem, the people lined the streets and cheered, much like they do during a parade today.

Line the children up on two sides. Explain that they are the crowd cheering for Jesus. Have the crowd practice *shouting: Hosanna!*

One at a time, let the children walk through the crowd with their donkey puppets. As the crowd cheers, their puppet *should call out "Braa-aaa-y!"*

Saying Goodbye:

Have the children put on their donkey puppets.

Say: A great way to share God's love in the world is by telling the stories of the Bible. Use your donkey puppets today to tell the story of Palm Sunday. Goodbye, Brady the Donkeys! Goodbye, Storytellers!

Snack:
crackers

grated cheese

Supplies:
(for Exploring Some More)

donkey puppets made earlier

119

Bible Verse:

"So they left the tomb quickly with fear and great joy, and ran to tell his disciples." (Matthew 28:8)

Supplies:

(for Opening a Gift Box)

box with lid

festive wrapping paper

bow

Story Eggs

Supplies:

(for Sharing a Story)

six plastic eggs

paper

markers or crayons

permanent marker

EASTER:
The Empty Tomb
Opening a Gift Box:

Cover a box and lid with festive wrapping paper. Add a bow to the lid. To introduce the message, put the Story Eggs into the box. (See Sharing a Story for directions on preparing the Story Eggs.)

Gather the children together. Hold up the gift box. Choose a child to take off the lid. Let the child tell everyone what's in the box. Next, hold up some of the Story Eggs.

Say: These are special Story Eggs. We will be using them in our Easter story today. We see lots of eggs at Easter time!

Ask: Where have you seen eggs this Easter? (*in my basket; We decorated eggs at school; My grandma brought me a china egg.*)

Say: Eggs are part of our Easter celebrations because eggs remind us that Jesus rose from the dead and left the tomb where he was buried. Birds and lots of other creatures come out, alive, from eggs. Jesus came out, alive, from the tomb.

Sharing a Story:

Create Story Eggs. Using a permanent marker, number the eggs from one to six. Then using markers or crayons, make simple sketches of the people or objects below:

> Egg 1: The Tomb
>
> Egg 2: The sun
>
> Egg 3: Two sad women
>
> Egg 4: An angel
>
> Egg 5: Two smiling faces of women
>
> Egg 6: Jesus and the two women.

Fold up each sketch and put it in the egg with the corresponding number.

The eggs will be placed in the gift box. The children will first see them in the opening activity, Opening a Gift Box.

The story is based on the account of the resurrection in Matthew 28:1-10.

As the story is told, invite a child to come up, pull out an egg, open the egg, unfold the sketch, and show it to the group. If there are more than six children, these tasks can be divided so that more than one child can be called forward at a time. Have each child or set of children return to their seats before moving on to the next egg.

Tell the Story:

> **Egg 1:** Jesus was put to death on a cross. His followers were very sad. They laid him to rest in a tomb.
>
> **Egg 2:** The sun was beginning to rise on Easter morning.
>
> **Egg 3:** Two women, Mary Magdalene and another woman named Mary, went to visit the tomb. They were sad because Jesus had died.
>
> **Egg 4:** Suddenly, there was a great earthquake. An angel of the Lord appeared and rolled back the stone door of the tomb. "Do not be afraid," the angel said to the women. Jesus has been raised from the dead. Come and see the place where he lay."

Egg 5: The women saw that Jesus was not in the tomb. They left quickly with fear and great joy.

Egg 6: All of a sudden, Jesus met them and said, "Greetings!" They took hold of his feet and worshiped him. Jesus told them, "Do not be afraid. Go tell the others that I will see them in Galilee." The women were very happy that Jesus was alive. They hurried to tell the others the good news.

Praying About the Tomb:

Have the children curl the fingers of one hand over the other to create an empty tomb.

Say: As I pray, look into the empty tomb you have created with your hands. Let us pray the Easter Prayer.

Exploring:

Children will create Surprise Eggs to surprise their family and friends.

Plan on three or four stickers per child. Cut the stickers apart ahead of time. Purchase small trinkets for the children to place in their eggs such as a smaller egg; a cross; or a chick, duck, frog, or other creature that hatches from an egg. Dollar stores and party stores are good places to search for the trinkets. If you cannot find trinkets, children can just decorate their eggs with stickers.

Give each child a plastic egg, stickers, and a trinket.

Say: When Jesus rose from the dead and came out of the tomb, the women were surprised. In honor of this surprise, you're going to make Surprise Eggs. The eggs will be plain on the outside, but when you open the top, there will be a surprise inside! You can have fun surprising people with your Surprise Egg.

Have them decorate the inside of the eggs with stickers, then tuck the trinket inside.

Say: When you show someone your Surprise Egg, first make them guess what is inside. Then let them open the top to see if their guess was correct.

Use a permanent marker to label the children's eggs with their names or initials.

Snacking From an Egg:

Surprise the children by tucking the snack into plastic eggs.

Say: Now I'm going to surprise you with your snack in an egg.

Ask: Can you guess what's inside? Do you think I put a watermelon in each egg? A hot dog? Spaghetti?

Let the children have fun guessing silly answers before serving the snack.

Exploring Some More:

Introduce the children to an old-fashioned Easter Game, "Egg on a Spoon."

Make a starting line and a line at the opposite end. Give each child a plastic or metal spoon. If you enjoyed a snack today, have each child use his or her plastic egg from the snack for the relay. If not, provide each child with a plastic egg.

When you **say: GO!** they are to walk (or run if outdoors) to the end line and back. Winners are those who do not let their eggs fall off the spoon.

Saying Goodbye:

Have the children hold their Surprise Eggs.

Say: An excellent way to share God's love is to tell others that Jesus died on the cross and then rose from the dead. As Christians, we celebrate the empty tomb. Goodbye, Christian Kids!

Easter Prayer:

God of Love, we celebrate the empty tomb of Easter. Thank you for raising Jesus from the dead. Amen.

Supplies:

(for Exploring)

plastic eggs

Easter stickers

small trinkets (see suggestions)

Snack:

plastic eggs (1 per child)

miniature cookies, pretzels, or yogurt-covered raisins

Supplies:

(for Exploring Some More)

plastic or metal spoons

plastic eggs (1 per child)

Verse:
"Let us come
into his
presence with
thanksgiving."
(Psalm 95:2)

Supplies:
(for Opening a
Gift Box)

box with lid

festive wrapping
paper

bow

Thanksgiving
greeting card,
table decoration,
or paper napkin

Supplies:
(for Sharing a
Story)

CD or tape of
the song
"Now Thank We
All Our God"

or choir member
to sing the song

THANKSGIVING:
Thankful Hearts
Opening a Gift Box:

Cover a box and a lid with festive wrapping paper. Add a bow to the lid. To introduce the message, place a Thanksgiving item inside the box.

Gather the children together. Hold up the gift box. Choose a child to take off the lid and hold up what is inside.

Ask: What's this? Does it remind you of a holiday? (*Thanksgiving*) What do you like to eat at Thanksgiving dinner? (*turkey, pumpkin pie, Grandma's green bean casserole*) What else do you enjoy doing on Thanksgiving Day? (*Going to see a parade; Playing with cousins; Helping cook dinner.*) Why do you we celebrate Thanksgiving? (*To thank God for our blessings; To remember the Pilgrims and the Native Americans who helped them.*)

Say: Since Bible days, people have been giving thanks to God for the harvest foods they grow and eat. Each day we thank God for food and other good gifts when we say grace before eating. In church, we sing our thanks to God with hymns such as "Praise God, from Whom All Blessings Flow." In the United States, the holiday we call "Thanksgiving" is a special day set aside for the whole country to give thanks. On Thanksgiving and every day, we should thank God with all our heart.

Sharing a Story:

Using words to a Thanksgiving hymn, the children will thank God with their heart and hands. You may want to play the hymn from a CD or tape, or have someone sing the hymn for the children after the story.

Tell the Story:

We are ready to thank God with our hands and our hearts as we act out the words to a song in the hymnal. The hymn is called "Now Thank We All Our God." It was written by a man named Martin Rinkart over three hundred years ago. Listen to the words and follow my hand motions.

> Now thank we all our God, with hearts (touch heart)
> And hands (wave hands)
> And voices, (touch mouth)
> Who wondrous things has done, (sweep arms over head)
> In whom this world rejoices; (wave arms and hands)
> Who from our mothers' arms (cradle right hand in left)
> Has blessed us on our way (move feet in place)
> With countless gifts of love, (extend both arms forward, palms up)
> And still is ours today. (both hands to chest)
>
> O may this bounteous God (raise both arms upwards)
> Through all our life be near us, (both hands to chest)
> With every joyful hearts (touch heart)
> And blessed peace to cheer us; (draw smile on lips)
> And keep us still in grace, (hug self)
> And guide us when perplexed; (shrug, with palms up)
> And free us from all ills, (sweep hands away from body)
> In this world and the next. (fold hands in prayer)
> All praise and thanks to God (raise both arms upwards)

The Father now be given; (raise both arms upwards)
The Son, and him who reigns (form cross with arms)
With them in highest heaven; (point upward)
The one eternal God, (hold up one finger)
Whom earth and heaven adore; (touch heart)
For thus it was, is now, (bring hands to left and then right)
And shall be evermore. (sweep arms over head and down)

If arrangements have been made for the children to hear the music, let them hear the hymn sung or played.

Say: On Thanksgiving, we especially thank God with our hearts (touch heart), our hands (wave hands), and our voices (lead all in *saying: Thank you God!*)

Praying About Thanksgiving:

Have the children put their hands on their hearts. Pray the Thanksgiving Prayer.

Exploring:

Celebrate blessings with a Giant Thankful Puzzle. If the group is large, consider making two puzzles, especially if the group will be doing the "Exploring Some More" activity.

Before Children's Church, print "Thank you God" around each of the four edges of the posterboard. Next, cut the poster into eight puzzle-shaped pieces of nearly equal size. Label the pieces: Family; Friends; Pets; Other Creatures; Foods; Plants; In the sky; On the earth.

Bring out the puzzle, unassembled, to a table. Holding up one piece at a time, ask each child to say what they are thankful for in that category. When all of the pieces have been discussed, invite the children to put the puzzle together.

Snacking With Thankfulness:

Feast on miniature Fruit Horns of Plenty. If practical, locate a picture of a traditional cornucopia, also called a "Horn of Plenty."

Begin by showing the picture to the children, explaining that the Horn of Plenty is a symbol of a good harvest of fruits and vegetables.

Give each child a cone and announce that this is now a miniature horn. Give them each a spoon, too. Invite them to fill their horns with plenty of fruit.

Before children eat their Horns of Plenty, lead them in *saying: Thank you, God, for these (name fruits) and for the food we eat each day! Amen.*

Exploring Some More:

Make the Giant Thankful Puzzle into a double-sided puzzle! Separate the puzzle into pieces, giving a piece to each child or pair of children. Read what is written on the piece and then turn it over. Invite the children to draw pictures to illustrate that category. When the drawings are finished, have the children reassemble the puzzle, showing the new side.

Say: With our words and our pictures, we thank God from our hearts.

Saying Goodbye:

Have everyone gather around the puzzle.

Say: One of the ways we share God's love on Thanksgiving is by being kind and helpful to others and by telling them how thankful we are that they are part of our lives. I am thankful to be with each of you! Goodbye, Thankful Hearts!

Thanksgiving Prayer:
God of Love,
we thank you for
everything you
have given us.
Help us to share
what we have
with others.
We love you.
Amen.

Supplies:
(for Exploring)
posterboard
a marker

Snack:
ice cream
sugar cones
(1 per child)
diced, fresh fruit
or canned
fruit cocktail
(well-drained)
spoons
picture of a
cornucopia

Supplies:
(for Exploring
Some More)
Giant Thankful
Puzzle(s) made in
Exploring
markers
crayons

Supplies:
(for Opening a Gift Box)

box with lid

festive wrapping paper, bow

angel ornament, decoration, or greeting card

Prayer:
God of Love, thank you for sending angels to tell Mary and Joseph the good news about the coming of baby Jesus. Amen.

Supplies:
(for Sharing a Story)

older children or teens to act out the story

costumes

124

ADVENT/CHRISTMAS:
Visiting Angels

Opening a Gift Box:

Cover a box and a lid with festive wrapping paper. Add a bow to the lid. To introduce the message, place an angel ornament, decoration, or greeting card in the box.

Gather the children. Choose a child to take off the lid and hold up what is inside.

Ask: What's this? (*an angel*) What holy book tells us stories about angels? (*The Bible*) Who sends angels to speak to people? (*God*)

Say: In the Bible, we read stories about people who are visited by angels. Angels tell messages from God. These messages help people know things that will happen.

Angels were created by God (Psalm 148:2-5). Angels lived before the creation of people (Job 38:4, 7). Angels do not get married, have children, or die (Luke 20:34-36). They have names (Luke 1:19). There are "ten thousands upon ten thousands" of them (Revelation 5:11). Angels worship God, and they help us by protecting, encouraging, and guiding us. They bring messages from God, and they help us understand what is happening. Angels appeared to Mary and Joseph to tell each of them about the birth of Jesus. Angels brought the news that Jesus was coming into the world!

Sharing a Story:

The story will be told using Scriptures from Luke 1:26-38 and Matthew 1:18-24.

If practical, invite older children or teens to pose for two tableau scenes: The Angel Gabriel with Mary, and the angel of the Lord appearing to Joseph. If no costumes are available, consider using robes, lengths of fabric, or bed sheets. Instruct the helpers to silently act out the events as the story is read.

Tell the Story:

In the Christmas story, the angel Gabriel visited Mary and an angel visited Joseph to tell them that Jesus would be born, and that they would be his parents.

Have the helpers, in costume, stand in front of the children for the first scene.

The angel Gabriel was sent to a town in Galilee called Nazareth. He visited a young woman named Mary. He said, "Greetings favored one! The Lord is with you." Then the angel said, "Do not be afraid, Mary, for you have found favor with God. You will have a son, and you will name him Jesus. He will be called the Son of God." Mary said, "Here I am. May it happen as you say."

Have the helpers change costumes, if need be.

An angel of the Lord appeared in a dream to Joseph, the man Mary was to marry. The angel said, "Joseph, do not be afraid to take Mary as your wife, for her child comes from the Holy Spirit. She will have a son, and you are to name him Jesus, for he will save his people from their sins." When Joseph woke up from his dream, he did as the angel told him, and took Mary to be his wife.

Thank any helpers who played a role in today's story.

Praying About Angels:

Have the children rest a hand on each of their hips and pretend that their arms are angel wings. Pray the Angel Prayer.

Exploring:

The children will make Tri-Fold Angel Centerpieces with a simple paper angel on each panel. (Each centerpiece requires two sheets of construction paper and three doilies.)

Prepare by folding and cutting the construction paper. Use a variety of colors.

Fold the paper into thirds across the width. Each one-third panel will measure 9- by 4-inches. Fold two sheets of paper per child. Next, unfold the sheets of paper and lay flat. Divide the paper into two equal stacks with a variety of colors in each stack.

Take one stack and cut each sheet of paper into thirds, using the creased fold line as a guide. Next, fold each of these strips in half lengthwise, so when folded they measure 2- by 9-inches. Measure up the fold 6 inches. Then, cut a triangle down from that point to the corner opposite the fold. When unfolded, these become the angels' robes.

From the remaining paper scraps, cut triangles measuring 2 inches wide by 2 inches long. These are the sleeves of the robes or the angels' wings. You will also need 1-inch round heads; make three for each centerpiece.

Make a sample to show the children. Place a sheet of the creased construction paper in front of you, so the fold lines are vertical. Glue a doily onto each of the three panels, with a margin of about one inch at the top. The doily creates a halo.

Choose three robe pieces in different colors. Glue each to a panel so the 4-inch robe base lines up across the width of the panel, with no margin. Next, glue on the smaller triangles, setting a point against each top side of the robe as shown. These become either the sleeves of the robes or the angels' wings.

Top each robe with an angel head. Add eyes and a smile. Consider adding some hair to the head and some decoration to the robe. Complete the centerpiece by taping the panels together at the top and bottom to make it free-standing.

Lead the children through the steps of creating their Tri-fold Angel Centerpiece. Explain that their centerpieces will make festive table decorations during Advent.

Snacking With Angels in Mind:

Serve holiday cookies on paper plates decorated with angels. Thank God for angels.

Exploring Some More:

Play a question game called "What Would Angels Say to Do?", similar to the famous question, "What would Jesus do?" The children will imagine what angels would say or do in various circumstances.

1. The kids in the neighborhood are upset about a boy who won't play fair. What would angels say to do?

2. A girl wants some money to buy Christmas gifts. She finds a wallet filled with money on the floor of a store. What would angels say to do?

3. You have toys you don't play with anymore even though they are very nice. What would angels say to do?

4. An elderly man at church is lonely. He never gets any mail or phone calls. What would angels say to do?

Saying Goodbye:

Have the children hold their Tri-fold Angel Centerpieces.

Say: We are glad that angels are a part of the Christmas Story. We can share God's love by telling others the story of the Christmas angels. Goodbye, Angel Artists!

construction paper (variety of colors)

3-inch, round paper doilies

ruler

glue

scissors

tape

markers or crayons

Snack:
Christmas cookies on angel plates

Message:

Mary and Joseph become the earthly parents to baby Jesus.

Verse:

"There was no place for them in the inn."
(Luke 2:7)

Supplies:

(for Opening a Gift Box)

box with lid

festive wrapping paper

bow

one or more baby items
(see suggestions)

ADVENT/CHRISTMAS:
Bethlehem Bound

Opening a Gift Box:

Cover a box and a lid with festive wrapping paper. Add a bow to the lid. Place one or more baby items in the box such as a toy, small piece of clothing, bib, cup, or spoon.

Gather the children. Choose a child to take off the lid and take out the baby item(s).

Ask: What's this? (*bib, rattle, baby cup*)

Say: When parents get ready for a baby, they gather items the baby will need.

Ask: What are some things that babies need? (*clothes, diapers, car seats*)

Say: In Bible times, people didn't have the fancy things we have for babies today. But they did have some things for babies such as clothes and simple toys. Since baby Jesus was on the way, Mary might have brought a few baby items with her when she left with Joseph to go to Bethlehem.

Sharing a Story:

The story, based on the Christmas story from Luke 2:1-7, tells why Mary and Joseph traveled to Bethlehem. Doors are mentioned often in this retelling. The Scriptures do not give the details of their trip, so some parts of the story are what may-have-been.

Tell the Story:

Today we'll pretend we are with Mary and Joseph as they make their trip to Bethlehem. Listen for the word "door." When you hear it, knock! (Depending on seating, have the children knock on the table, a chair, or the floor.)

One day, Joseph heard a knock on his DOOR. (knock) A Roman soldier stood outside with the news that the Emperor wanted everyone in the Roman Empire to be counted. The orders said that people must go to their hometowns and be counted there. Joseph's hometown was in Bethlehem.

Joseph walked to Mary's home and knocked on the DOOR. (knock) He told her the news and said that she would go with him to Bethlehem, since they would soon be married.

Mary began preparing for the trip. She packed baby clothes. She packed dried raisins, dates, nuts, cheese, and homemade flatbread. Then she knocked on the DOORS (knock) of her family and the DOORS (knock) of her friends to say farewell.

Joseph knocked on the stable master's DOOR (knock/pause), and asked to buy a donkey. He chose a strong, gentle donkey to carry the supplies and to carry Mary, too.

At the DOOR (knock) of Mary's house, her parents gave the couple some money.

At the DOOR (knock) of Joseph's house, his parents gave them a bag of special medicinal herbs and a beautiful baby blanket.

On the first day of their trip, they made it to the town of Nam. Joseph knocked on the DOOR (knock) of a cousin, who gave them supper and a place to sleep.

The next day, they knocked at the DOOR (knock) of an inn, where they slept.

The next night, they had no DOORS (knock) to knock on, but a shepherd shared his campfire and some food with them.

After walking many miles, Joseph told Mary that he could see Bethlehem just ahead.

Mary told Joseph that she was very tired and asked him to knock on the first DOOR (knock) he saw. The streets of Bethlehem were crowded with other travelers,

126

but Joseph knocked at the DOORS (knock) of all the inns. He knocked on the DOORS (knock) of all the shops. He even knocked on the DOORS (knock) of the bigger houses. But no one had a place for them to stay.

Finally, an innkeeper saw them pass by again. He could see that Mary was expecting a baby and that Joseph looked worried. The innkeeper said they could stop knocking on DOORS (knock) because they could stay in his stable. Mary and Joseph were thankful. Not long after they arrived in Bethlehem, baby Jesus was born.

Praying About Mary and Joseph:

Lead the children in the prayer, with one more knock. Pray.

Exploring:

Children will make Door Ornaments in honor of Mary and Joseph. Although not necessary, small buttons for doorknobs can be used. Use caution in giving buttons to very young children.

Before Children's Church, print "Luke 2:7" on each index card.

Make a sample ornament to show the children. Turn the card so the five-inch side is vertical. Tape a six-inch loop of yarn or ribbon to the middle of the top edge of the card to form a hanger for the Christmas ornament. Next, on the side of the card that has no writing on it, line up the craft sticks, side by side, enough to cover the card and to create the look of a wooden door. (The craft sticks will be lengthwise.) Glue the sticks in place. Add a small, flat button for a doorknob.

Give each child a card, and set out the other supplies. Show the sample to the children. Read the Bible verse, explaining that "Luke 2:7" is where today's verse is found in the Bible. Guide the children through the steps of making the ornament.

Say: When you see this ornament on your Christmas tree, you will remember Mary and Joseph and the trip they made to Bethlehem.

Snacking Like Travelers:

Serve individual boxes of raisins and/or cheese cubes and crackers. Explain to the children that there were no fast food places or snack machines in Bible times. Mary and Joseph had to bring food such as this on their journey.

Exploring Some More:

Here are some choices for extending the lesson.

1) Invite the children to tell stories of their travels near and far. Ask their opinions on car seats, traffic, car snacks, and more.

2) In a large room or up and down a hallway, reenact the story by pretending to pack, buy a donkey, walk, sit by a campfire, knock on doors, and settle into the stable.

Saying Goodbye:

Have the children hold their Door Ornaments.

Say: We are thankful for Mary and Joseph and thankful to God, who finds many ways to share love with us. Goodbye, Kids of Love!

Prayer:
God of Love, we knock on your DOOR (knock) to say "thank you" for choosing Mary and Joseph to be the parents of Jesus. Amen.

Supplies:
(for Exploring)
NRSV Bible
3- by 5-inch index cards
small craft sticks
marker
glue
yarn or ribbon
scissors
tape
(optional) small, flat buttons

Snack:
individual boxes of raisins and/or cheese cubes and crackers

Verse:

"Let us go now to Bethlehem and see this thing that has taken place." (Luke 2:15)

Supplies:

(for Opening a Gift Box)

box with lid

festive wrapping paper

bow

sheep toy, ornament, figure from a nativity set, or Christmas card

ADVENT/CHRISTMAS:
Shepherds' Watch
Opening a Gift Box:

Cover a box and a lid with festive wrapping paper. Add a bow to the lid. Put a sheep toy, ornament, figure from a nativity set, or Christmas card picture into the box.

Gather the children. Choose a child to open the box and pull out what is inside.

Ask: What's this? (*a sheep*) Who watches over sheep to keep them safe? (*shepherds*) Where do shepherds spend a lot of time with sheep? (*in the fields*)

Say: When baby Jesus was born in Bethlehem, some shepherds were on a field outside of town. These shepherds were not rich or famous, but God sent an angel to them. The angel told the shepherds that a child was born in Bethlehem who was the Savior and the Messiah. Believing the angel, the good shepherds walked in the dark of night to look for baby Jesus. And they found him!

Because God loves the people of the world, God sent Jesus. God shared the news with the shepherds and let them be some of the very first people to see baby Jesus.

Sharing a Story:

In this retelling of the story of the Christmas shepherds (Luke 2:8-19), the children will participate by raising candy canes and *saying: We're the shepherds!*

Tell the Story:

These may look like holiday treats (hand out candy canes), but during our story, they will become shepherds' staffs! When you hear the word "shepherds" in the story, hold up your staff and *say: We're the shepherds!* Let's practice a few times.

In the fields outside the town of Bethlehem, SHEPHERDS (pause) were sitting around a campfire. The SHEPHERDS (pause) played their flutes and talked quietly. Fluffy sheep slept in the grass nearby. The night sky was filled with stars. The SHEPHERDS (pause) pulled their wool blankets around them. They were just about to lay down, when a great burst of light shone all around them.

"SHEPHERDS!" (pause) said the angel of the Lord.

The SHEPHERDS (pause) began shaking with fear and surprise.

"Do not be afraid," said the angel, "for see—I am bringing you good news of great joy for all the people: to you is born this day in the city of David a Savior, who is the Messiah, the Lord."

The SHEPHERDS (pause) smiled.

The angel explained where to find the Savior, saying, "This will be a sign for you: you will find a child wrapped in bands of cloth and lying in a manger."

The SHEPHERDS (pause) nodded their heads.

Suddenly there appeared lots and lots of angels around the angel of the Lord. The heavenly angels praised God saying, "Glory to God in the highest heaven, and on earth peace."

The SHEPHERDS' (pause) mouths dropped open in amazement.

Then the angels went back to heaven, leaving the darkness of night over the fields.

The SHEPHERDS (pause) said to one another, "Let us go to Bethlehem and see this thing that has taken place, which the Lord has made known to us."

Supplies:

(for Sharing a Story)

candy cane (any size) (1 per child)

Across the fields and over the road walked the SHEPHERDS (pause). They looked up one street and down another until they found Mary, Joseph, and the baby.

When the SHEPHERDS (pause) saw Jesus, they told Mary and Joseph and everyone at the stable about the angels and their message. All who heard the SHEPHERDS' (pause) story were amazed.

The SHEPHERDS (pause) returned to their fields, praising God for all they had seen and heard on that wonderful night.

Praying About Shepherds:

Have the children raise their candy canes in the air during the Shepherds' Prayer.

Exploring:

Children will make Shepherds' Staffs. They can make as many staffs as time and supplies permit.

Before Children's Church, make a sample staff to show them. Each staff is fashioned from one chenille stem. Fold and bring the stem ends together, pressing the two stem lengths side by side. Twist the ends together tightly along the length. Bend the staff at one end.

Pass around the sample Shepherd's Staff. Next, show the children how to make their own. Explain that they can use their staffs to help decorate their Christmas tree or display them in other places in their home.

Snacking on Shepherds' Staffs:

Before Children's Church or with the children, shape canned dough into staffs before baking. The children may eat their candy canes from the storytime, too.

As they enjoy the snack, lead them in singing this song, set to the tune of "Angel Band" or "Ten Little Indians."

> **Sing:** There was one, there were two, there were three little shepherds,
> There were four, there were five, there were six little shepherds,
> There were seven, there were eight, there were nine little shepherds,
> Ten little shepherds in the field!

Exploring Some More:

Now it's time to play "Search for the Manger." This can be done on a large or small scale. If it is possible to wander the halls and other rooms during Children's Church, wrap a baby doll in a blanket and place the doll in a location that requires a bit of a hike. Have the children *say: We're the shepherds looking for a baby* as they enter each hallway or room in search of the baby.

On a smaller scale, borrow a baby in a manger from a nativity set and hide the baby in a room. March with the children around the room one time, *saying: We're the shepherds on a shepherds' search!* Then let your shepherds search for the baby in a manger figure.

Saying Goodbye:

Have the children hold their Shepherds' Staffs.

Say: God shared love with the shepherds by sending the angel with the good news of the birth of Jesus. God wanted these ordinary people to be among the first to see the baby Jesus. During Christmas, let's try to search for goodness and kindness and do our best to tell good news! Goodbye, Sweet Shepherds!

Prayer:
God of Love, we like to pretend that we are the shepherds who heard the angels' good news, looked for the baby in the manger, and felt great joy when they found Jesus. Amen.

Supplies:
(for Exploring)
chenille stems

Snack:
canned breadstick or sugar cookie dough
candy canes

ADVENT/CHRISTMAS:
Jesus Is Born!

Opening a Gift Box:

Bible Verse:

"Now the birth of Jesus the Messiah took place in this way." (Matthew 1:18)

Cover a box and a lid with festive wrapping paper. Add a bow to the lid. To introduce the message, put an artist's rendering of the infant Jesus into the box. Look for a picture in a Bible storybook, a nativity figure, or a Christmas card that portrays the baby Jesus.

Gather the children together. Hold up the gift box. Choose a child to open the box and pull out what is inside.

Ask: Who is this? (*baby Jesus*) Why do we see pictures /figures of baby Jesus, especially at this time of the year? (*Because God sent him to us. Because Christmas is about Jesus' birth. Because Jesus is the Savior.*)

Say: Christmas is the day we celebrate the birth of Jesus. We sing songs, tell stories, and put on plays about the birth of Jesus. We have special activities at church, we decorate our homes, and we make holiday food because we are joyful.

Supplies:
(for Opening a Gift Box)

box with lid

festive wrapping paper

bow

images of baby Jesus

We do all this because this little baby (point to baby Jesus) became a great and holy man. He was an amazing preacher, healer, and teacher. Most important of all, Jesus was the Savior. Jesus came to talk to us about God and heaven, to teach us the right ways to act, and to forgive us for the wrong things we do. Jesus Christ is our Savior, and we remember his birth on Christmas Day.

Sharing a Story:

Bringing together the Gospel accounts that lead to the birth of Jesus, this story is told using a nativity set. If there is not a nativity set handy, use Christmas cards that show angels, Mary and Joseph, shepherds, and baby Jesus. (The wise men were not present at Jesus' birth.)

Tell the Story:

(This is a nativity set/these are Christmas cards) that help us imagine the characters in the Christmas story and the events that took place leading to the birth of Jesus. Listen, as each one tells what happened.

Hold up each character during his or her part of the story.

Angel: I am an angel. Angels are sent by God with messages for people on earth. The angel Gabriel explained to Mary that she had been chosen by God to be the mother of Jesus. An angel told Joseph that Mary was expecting a very special baby, and that he should be her husband and a father to baby Jesus. On the night that Jesus was born, an angel of the Lord brought the good news to shepherds in a field. Then a multitude of angels came too, to praise God. The birth of Jesus gave great joy to the angels of heaven. We angels share God's love with the world.

Joseph: I am Joseph. One night I had an unbelievable dream. An angel came to me and told me about the future. The angel said that Mary was going to have a baby. The baby was sent by God. The angel told me I should not be afraid to marry Mary. I must name her baby, Jesus, because Jesus would one day save the people from their sins. When I woke up, I did all that the angel told me to do. I will be a good father to baby Jesus and share in God's love for the world.

Mary: I am Mary. While I was engaged to be married to a wonderful man named Joseph, the angel Gabriel came to me. The angel told me not to be afraid because I had been chosen by God. I did not understand, so the angel helped me see that I was to be the mother of a holy child. I shared God's love for the world by giving birth to God's Son.

Shepherds: We are shepherds. One evening, we were camped outside of Bethlehem when we got the biggest surprise of our lives! An angel of the Lord appeared before us in a great burst of light, saying not to be afraid. Of course, we were shaking anyway. This angel told us that on that very day the Savior had been born. After telling us the good news, the angel told us to go to Bethlehem and find this baby, who would be sleeping on hay. It was dark, but we went to town right away. We were so happy to see the child. We told everyone about that night. We certainly shared in God's love for the world.

Baby: Waa! I'm baby Jesus. From my manger crib I see my mother Mary and my father Joseph. I feel the love of all those around me. I am a part of God's love for the world.

Praying About Baby Jesus:

Show the children how to cradle their arms as if they are holding a baby. Pray the Baby Jesus Prayer.

Exploring:

Children will make their very own Baby Jesus Clothespin Ornaments. (If you cannot find miniature craft clothespins, use regular-sized clothespins and larger strips of cloth.)

Before Children's Church, prepare a clothespin for each child. First, use the marker to draw eyes and a smile on the round head of each clothespin. Next, use the paint pen or glitter pen to paint a halo around the top of the head.

Cut strips of cloth to be swaddled around the clothespin figures. Cut six-inch lengths of yarn or ribbon to tie around the swaddling.

Give each child a prepared clothespin doll and lay out the cloth strips and yarn or ribbon.

Say: To celebrate the birth of Jesus, we are going to make Baby Jesus Clothespin Ornaments. Each of you has a smiling baby with a halo. The Bible tells us that Mary wrapped baby Jesus with bands of cloth. Now you are going to wrap your baby with bands of cloth.

Show the children how to wrap a strip of cloth around the clothespin doll. Have them experiment with wrapping and rewrapping until they are satisfied with the results. Ask them to hold the cloth in place while you tie yarn or ribbon around the baby. Tell the children that when they get home, a wire ornament hanger can be hooked to the back of the ribbon so they can put the ornament on their Christmas tree.

When the clothespin dolls are finished, have the children hold them in the palm of their hands. Sing or say a verse of "Away in a Manger" as they rock their babies.

Sing: Away in a manger, no crib for a bed,
The little Lord Jesus laid down his sweet head.
The stars in the sky looked down where he lay,
The little Lord Jesus, asleep on the hay.

Baby Jesus Prayer:
God of Love,
thank you
for sending
baby Jesus,
who would grow
up to be
our Savior.
Amen.

Supplies:
(for Exploring)

miniature craft clothespins

1- by 4-inch strips of cloth (1 per child)

yarn or ribbon

scissors

a fine-tip marker, a gold or silver paint pen, or a glitter pen

Snack:

chow mein noodles
or no-bake
cookie recipe

12 ounces of
butterscotch chips

cooking oil
or butter

parchment paper,
wax paper, or foil

cookie sheet
microwavable bowl
pot holders

Supplies:
(for Exploring
Some More)

CD or tape of
children's
Christmas music

children's
Christmas book
such as,
*Unwrapping the
Christmas Crèche*

Snacking on Manger Hay:

Serve the children plain chow mein noodles, or make Haystacks using this no-bake cookie recipe.

Line a baking sheet with waxed paper, parchment, or foil. Spray with cooking oil or rub with butter. Evenly distribute six ounces of chow mein noodles over the surface.

In a microwave, melt 12 ounces of butterscotch chips. Drizzle the melted butterscotch chips over the noodles, coating thoroughly. When the noodles are completely cooled, break them apart into small haystacks.

Exploring Some More:

Enjoy a Christmas Sing-a-long! Play the music, encouraging everyone to sing along. Don't be shy—lift up your voice and rejoice.

The children will enjoy hearing a story based on a nativity set, *Unwrapping the Christmas Crèche,* by Lisa Flinn and Barbara Younger (Abingdon Press, ISBN: 9780687497836) After reading the story, ask them to describe their own nativity sets, if they have one.

Saying Goodbye:

Have the children hold their Baby Jesus Clothespin Ornaments.

Say: Merry Christmas! God shared great love for the world by sending Jesus to the earth. We love the baby Jesus. Goodbye, Christmas Kids!